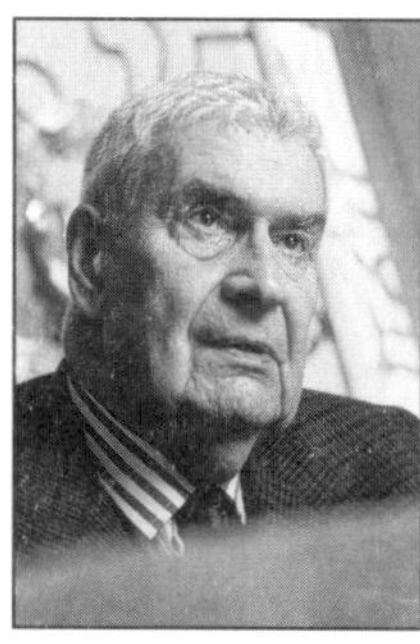

FEDERICO ZERI (Rome, 1921-1998), eminent art historian and critic, was vice-president of the National Council for Cultural and Environmental Treasures from 1993. Member of the Académie des Beaux-Arts in Paris, he was decorated with the Legion of Honor by the French government. Author of numerous artistic and literary publications; among the most well-known: *Pittura e controriforma*, the Catalogue of Italian Painters in the Metropolitan Museum of New York and the Walters Gallery of Baltimora, and the book *Confesso che ho sbagliato*.

Work edited by FEDERICO ZERI

Text
based on the interviews between
FEDERICO ZERI and MARCO DOLCETTA

This edition is published for North America in 1999 by NDE Publishing*

Chief Editor of 1999 English Language Edition
ELENA MAZOUR (*NDE Publishing**)

English Translation
MARK EATON FOR SCRIPTUM S.R.L.

Realisation
CONFUSIONE S.R.L., ROME

Editing
ISABELLA POMPEI

Desktop Publishing
SIMONA FERRI, KATHARINA GASTERSTADT

ISBN 1-55321-002-6

Illustration references

Alinari archives: 37b.

Bridgeman/Alinari archives: 14b, 15tl, 22, 37t, 39b, 40c, 43, 45/XI.

Giraudon/Alinari archives: 10b, 12bl, 13br, 23, 33t, 36, 38tr, 44/VI, 45/ VII.

Luisa Ricciarini Agency: 1, 2-3, 4, 5, 6-7, 8l-tr, 9 10t-r, 10-11, 12c-br, 12-13t, 18, 19, 29, 38-39, 42b, 45/II-IV.

RCS Libri Archives: 2t, 8b, 12t, 14t, 15tc-tr, 15bl-bc, 16tl-c, 17cr, 20, 21, 24, 27t-c -br, 28t-b, 31, 32, 34b, 34-35, 36t, 42t, 44/II-III-V-VII-IX-X-XII, 45/I-VI-IX-X-XIII-XIV, 47.

R.D.: 2b, 10tl, 12-13b, 13t, 15br, 16tr, 16-17b, 17t-cl-b, 25, 26, 27bl, 28c, 30, 33b, 34t, 38tl-bl, 40t-b, 41, 44/I-IV-VIII-XI, 45/III-V-VIII-XII.

Printed and bound by Poligrafici Calderara S.p.A., Bologna, Italy

* *a registred business style of NDE Canada Corp.*
18-30 Wertheim Court, Richmond Hill, Ontario
L4B 1B9 Canada, tel. (905) 731-12 88

The captions of the paintings contained in this volume include, beyond just the title of the work, the dating and location. In the cases where this data is missing, we are dealing with works of uncertain dating, or whose current whereabouts are not known. The titles of the works of the artist to whom this volume is dedicated are in blue and those of other artists are in red.

VAN GOGH
STARRY NIGHT

STARRY NIGHT is dominated by the crescent moon at the top right, the large stars and the turbulent air, while the landscape opens up behind a wing made up of huge cypresses. It is an extremely significant work,

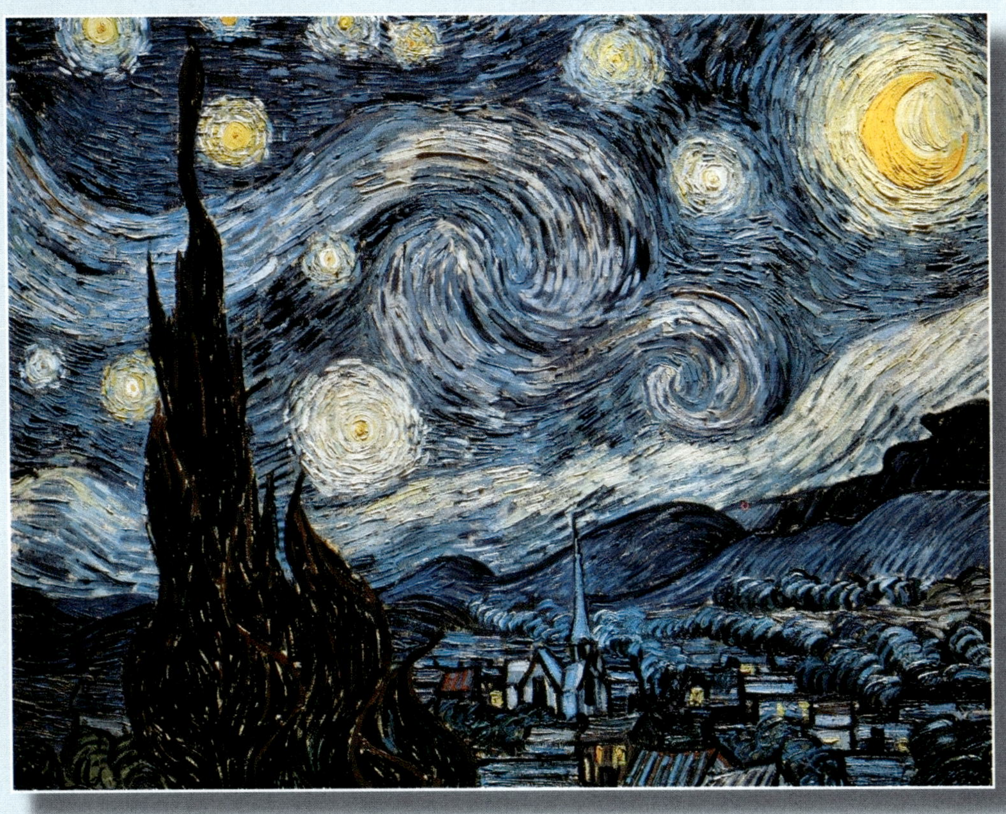

both in terms of technique and of the use of color. The brush-strokes, laid one next to the other like a mosaic, give the whole work a sense of incessant movement. The undulant rhythm that pervades it demonstrates an undeniable link with Art Nouveau.

THE LANDSCAPE OF THE SOUL

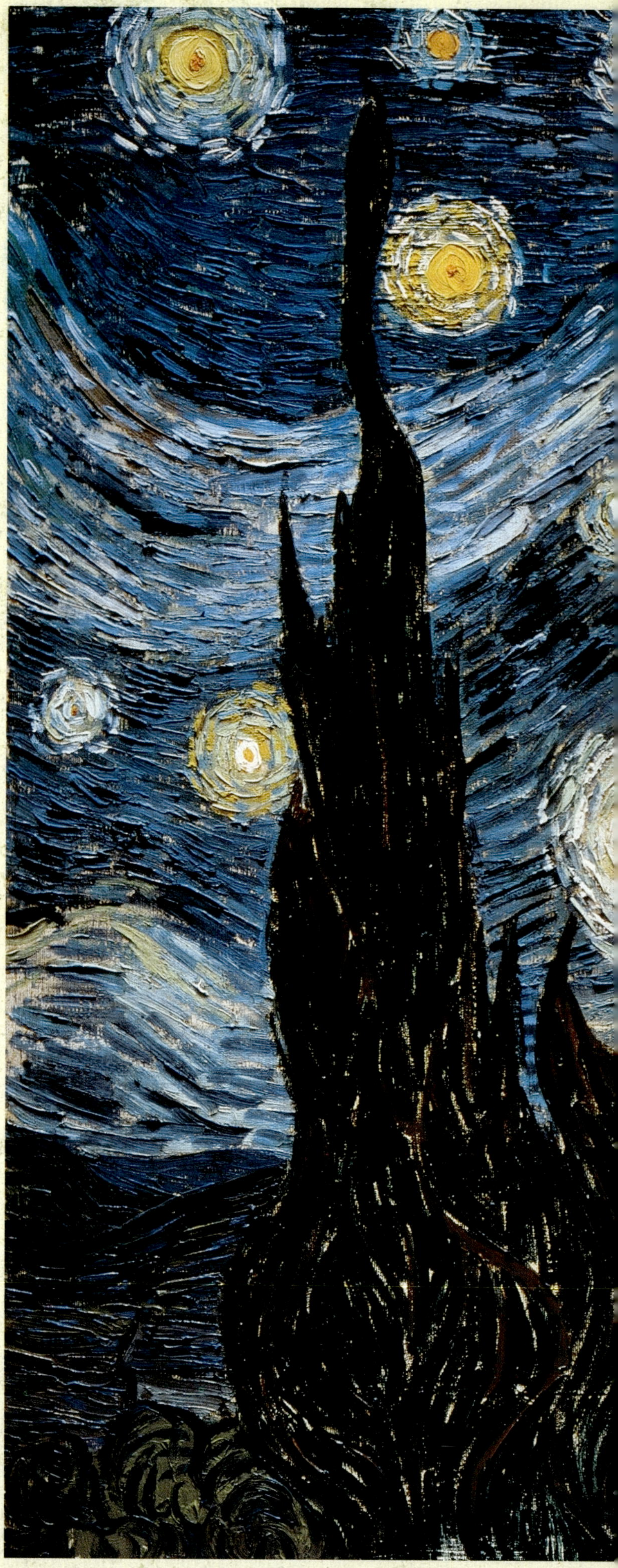

STARRY NIGHT

June 1889

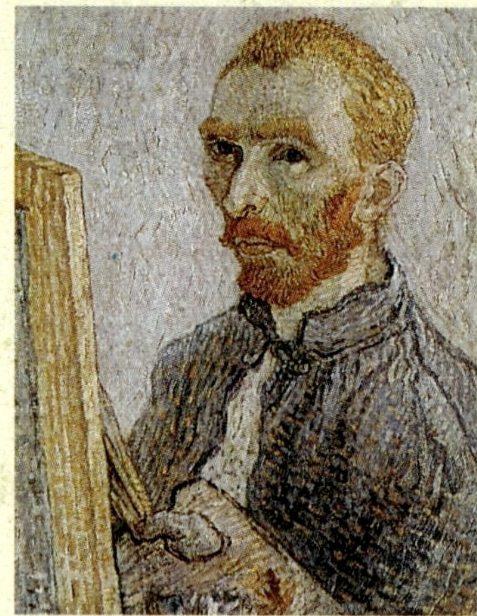

- New York, Museum of Modern Art (oil on canvas, 73 x 92 cm)
- *Starry Night* was painted in June 1889 in Saint-Rémy de Provence, where Van Gogh had been staying since May. After cutting off his ear, in December 1888, he had spent a long period in the hospital at Arles before deciding to go into the Saint-Paul de Mausole asylum for mental illnesses.
- From the window of his room he could admire the wheat fields, the olives groves and the cypresses, and in these arid, sun-drenched landscapes he managed to find the relief and comfort to react to his difficulties.
- In the intervals between his attacks of mental illness, he made copies from prints of masterpieces such as those of Millet and also landscapes views based partly on memory and partly on direct observation. His canvases were animated by sudden vortexes of color, and a previously unseen dynamism filled his landscapes with a febrile energy that expressed a new, heightened vision.
- His compositions, now extremely simplified, were arranged in a rising rhythm, while the expressive freedom of the brushstrokes reduced the mimetic faithfulness. Van Gogh was pouring his own suffering into his landscapes, looking for "a type of painting that can bring greater consolation". Painting came increasingly to signify salvation: by describing the surrounding reality, Van Gogh escaped from the tragedy of the asylum.

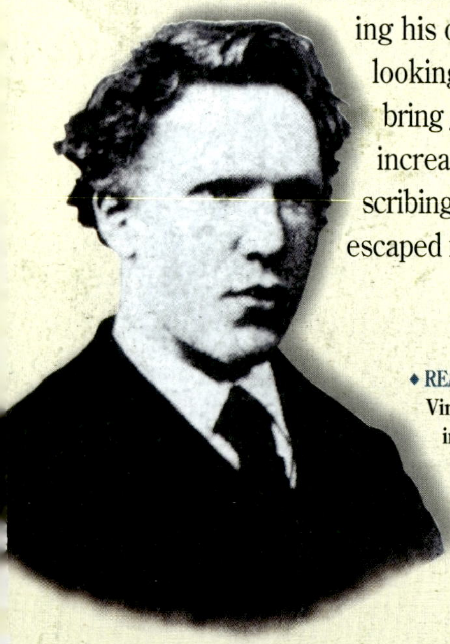

◆ **REALITY AND ART** Vincent Van Gogh in a photo taken in 1871 (left). In the asylum in Saint-Rémy, he was forced to stay in his room for long spells, and could only paint self-portraits, including the one at the top of the page.

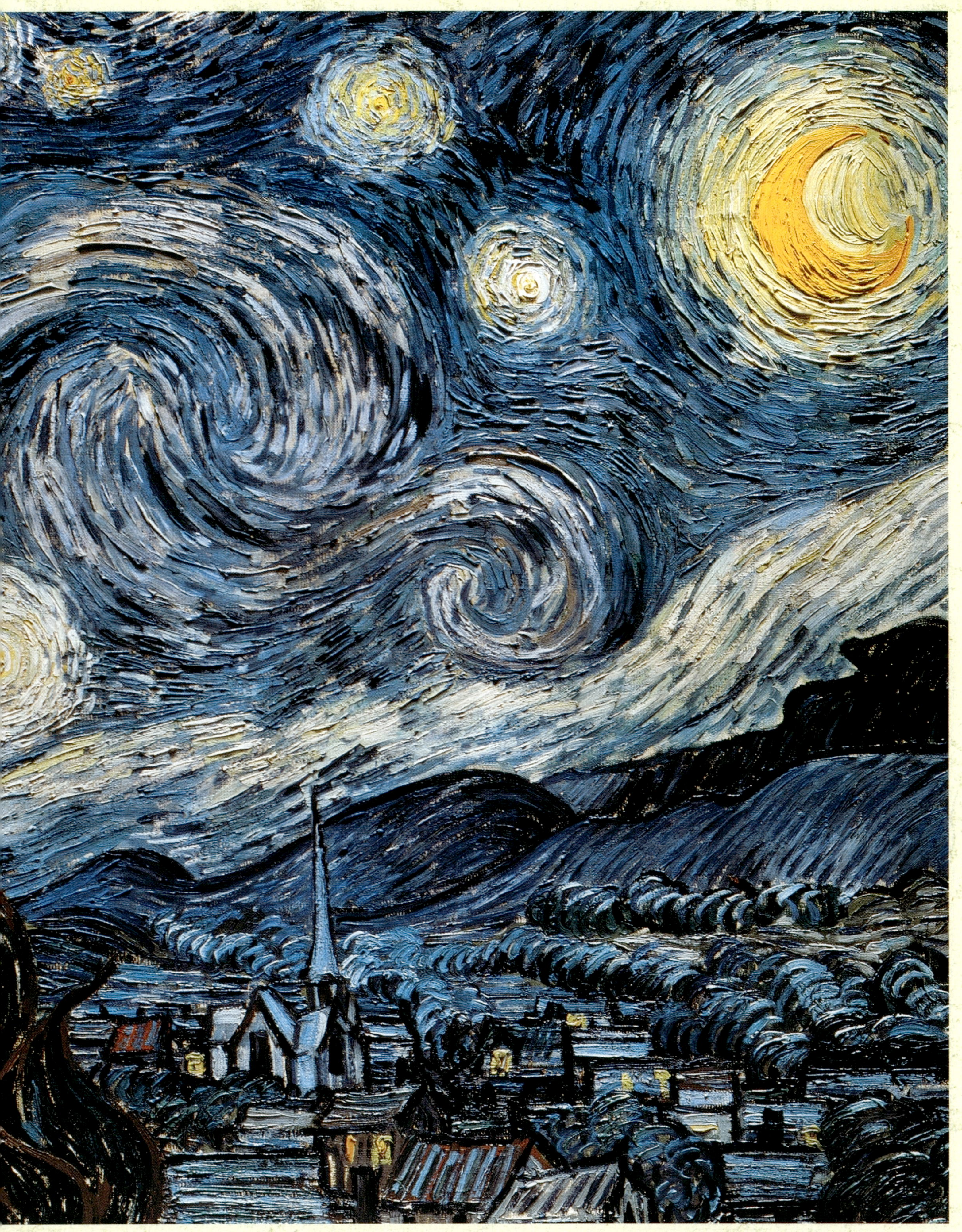

A COSMIC PARABLE

In *Starry Night*, Van Gogh continues to work from memory rather than from observation: the canvas is born, in fact, from his nostalgic recollection of the landscapes of Northern Europe. Here his memory turns to the villages of his native land, the steeples that rise to challenge the sky and the peace of the surrounding houses, absorbed by the regular rhythm of life. The nocturnal silence of the village is, however, shattered by the pyrotechnic display of the sky and by the flame-like cypresses. The darting brush-strokes animate the whole surface of the canvas.

● In this reworking of real and imagined sources, Van Gogh achieves a surprising effect of abstraction. He reduces the shapes to pure outlines, and the palette to the primary colors. Blues and yellows thus meet to evoke the green of the land, but spread arbitrarily over the forms without the slightest respect for faithful mimesis. The sky and the earth merge together to express an anxious sense of infinity and immensity.

● The world seems to be melting as if it were made of wax. Van Gogh abolishes three-dimensionality and the confines between objects. All the volumes are absorbed into the convulsive rhythm of thick, though brief brush-strokes which, like continuous waves, convey a tension that is not merely visual but also emotional.

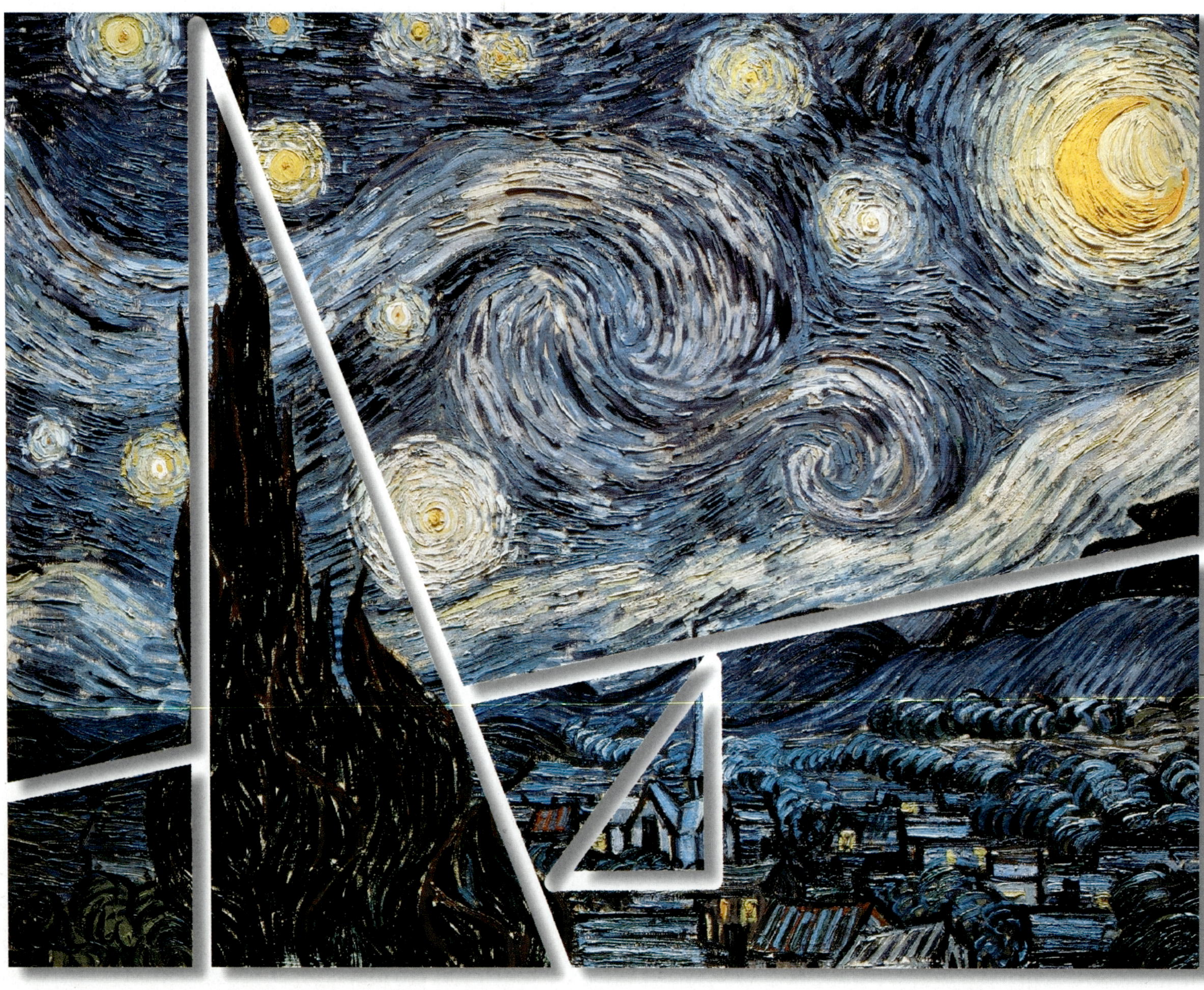

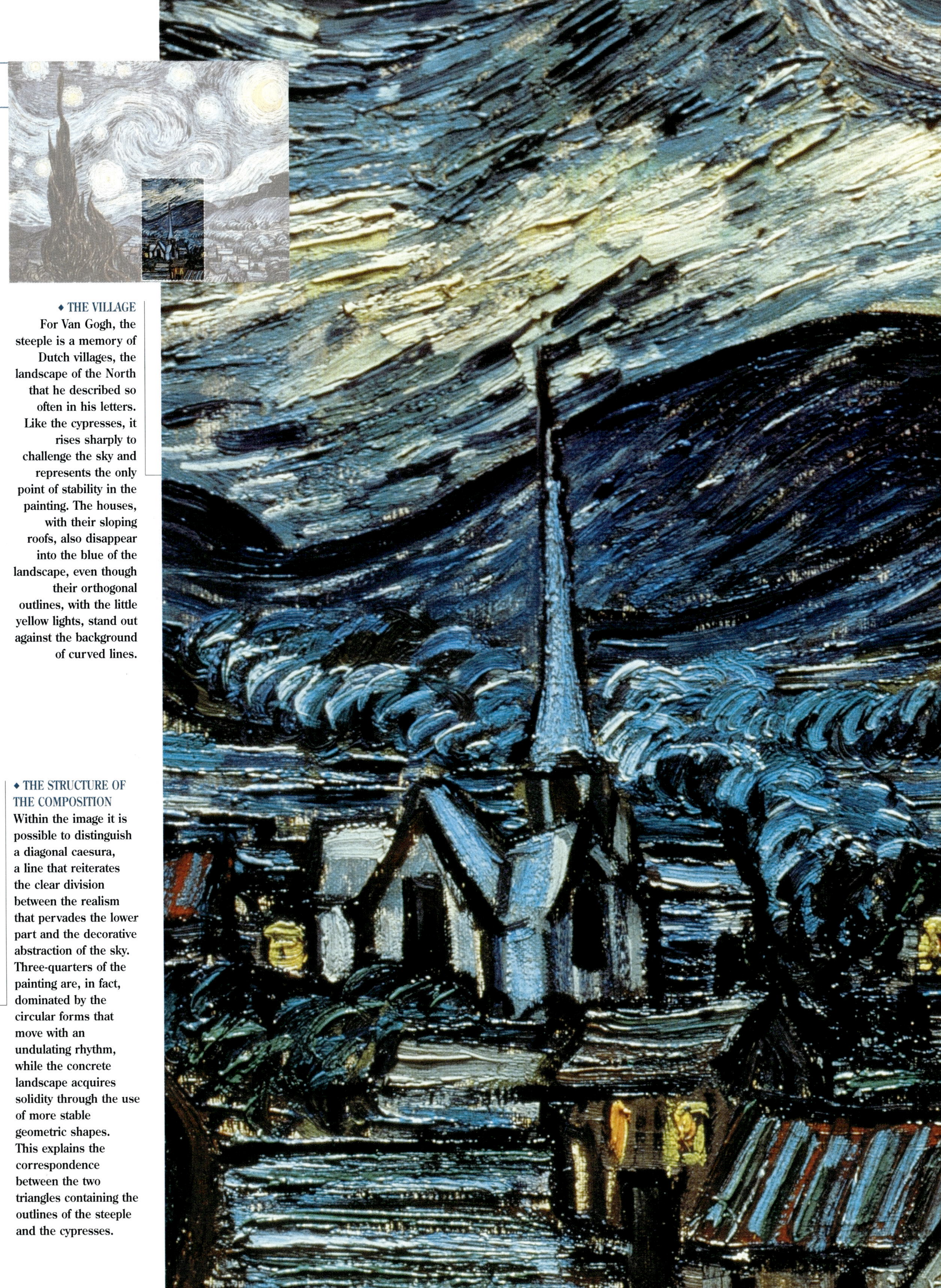

◆ THE VILLAGE
For Van Gogh, the steeple is a memory of Dutch villages, the landscape of the North that he described so often in his letters. Like the cypresses, it rises sharply to challenge the sky and represents the only point of stability in the painting. The houses, with their sloping roofs, also disappear into the blue of the landscape, even though their orthogonal outlines, with the little yellow lights, stand out against the background of curved lines.

◆ THE STRUCTURE OF THE COMPOSITION
Within the image it is possible to distinguish a diagonal caesura, a line that reiterates the clear division between the realism that pervades the lower part and the decorative abstraction of the sky. Three-quarters of the painting are, in fact, dominated by the circular forms that move with an undulating rhythm, while the concrete landscape acquires solidity through the use of more stable geometric shapes. This explains the correspondence between the two triangles containing the outlines of the steeple and the cypresses.

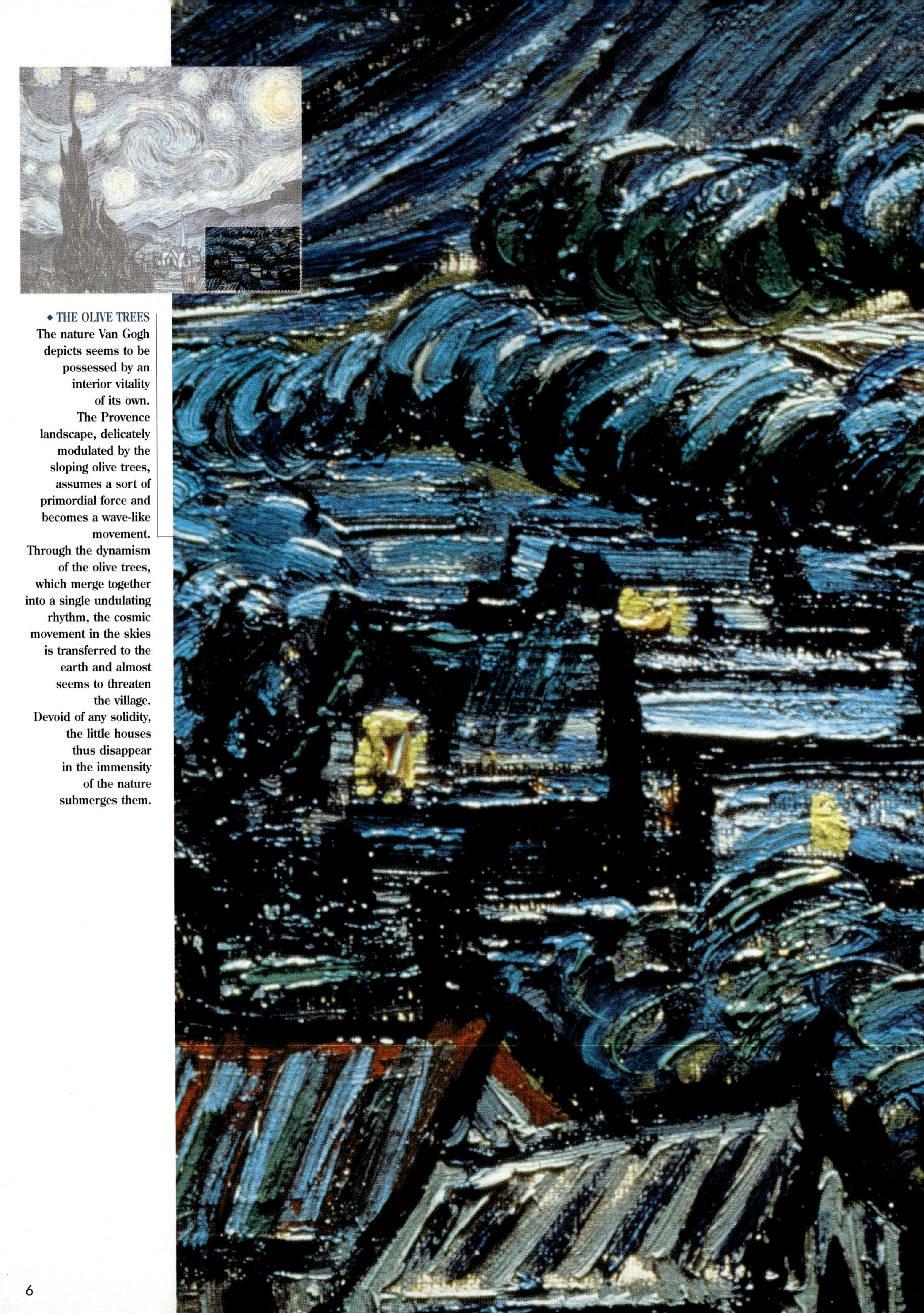

◆ THE OLIVE TREES
The nature Van Gogh depicts seems to be possessed by an interior vitality of its own. The Provence landscape, delicately modulated by the sloping olive trees, assumes a sort of primordial force and becomes a wave-like movement. Through the dynamism of the olive trees, which merge together into a single undulating rhythm, the cosmic movement in the skies is transferred to the earth and almost seems to threaten the village. Devoid of any solidity, the little houses thus disappear in the immensity of the nature submerges them.

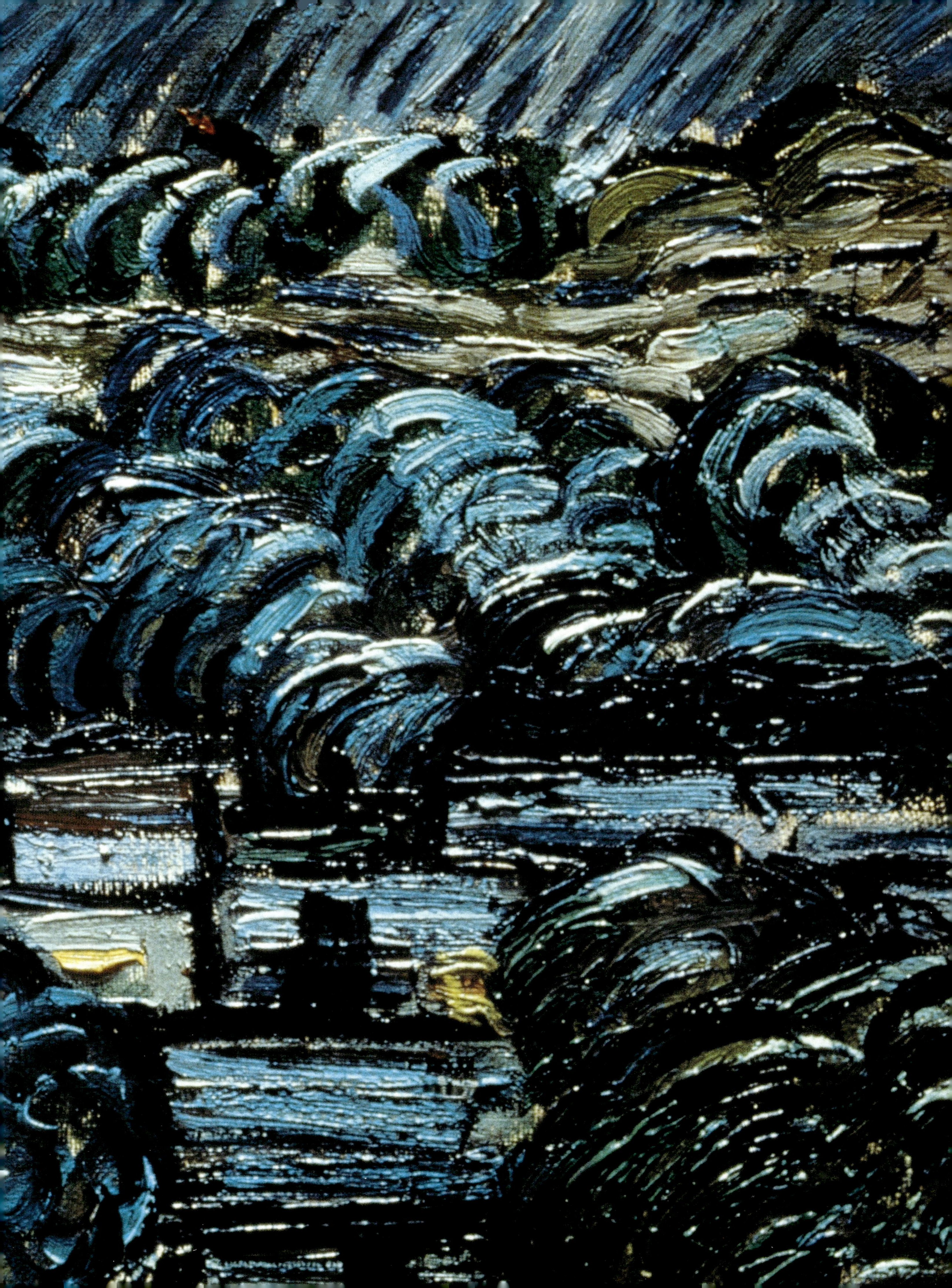

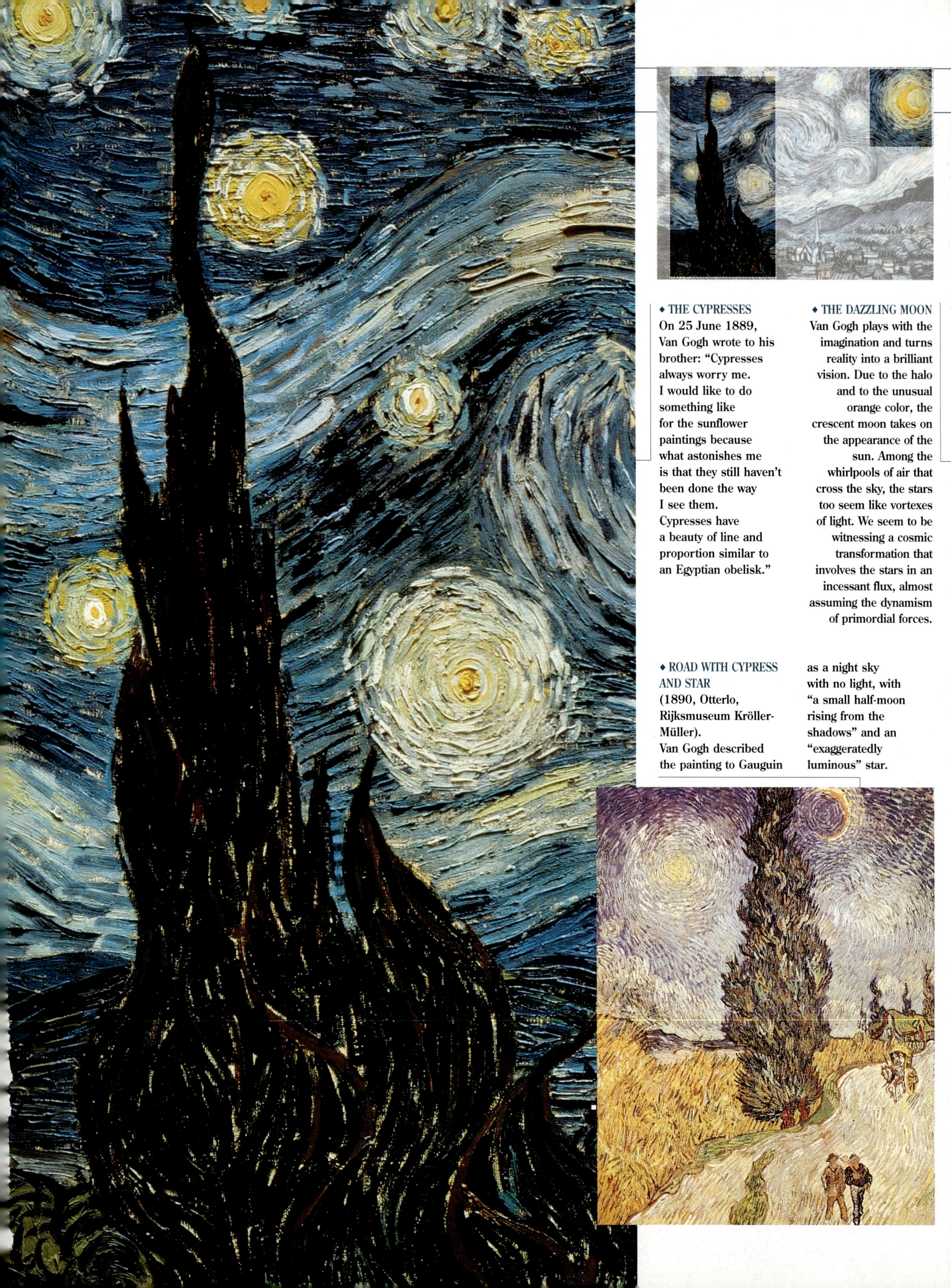

◆ THE CYPRESSES
On 25 June 1889, Van Gogh wrote to his brother: "Cypresses always worry me. I would like to do something like for the sunflower paintings because what astonishes me is that they still haven't been done the way I see them. Cypresses have a beauty of line and proportion similar to an Egyptian obelisk."

◆ THE DAZZLING MOON
Van Gogh plays with the imagination and turns reality into a brilliant vision. Due to the halo and to the unusual orange color, the crescent moon takes on the appearance of the sun. Among the whirlpools of air that cross the sky, the stars too seem like vortexes of light. We seem to be witnessing a cosmic transformation that involves the stars in an incessant flux, almost assuming the dynamism of primordial forces.

◆ ROAD WITH CYPRESS AND STAR
(1890, Otterlo, Rijksmuseum Kröller-Müller).
Van Gogh described the painting to Gauguin as a night sky with no light, with "a small half-moon rising from the shadows" and an "exaggeratedly luminous" star.

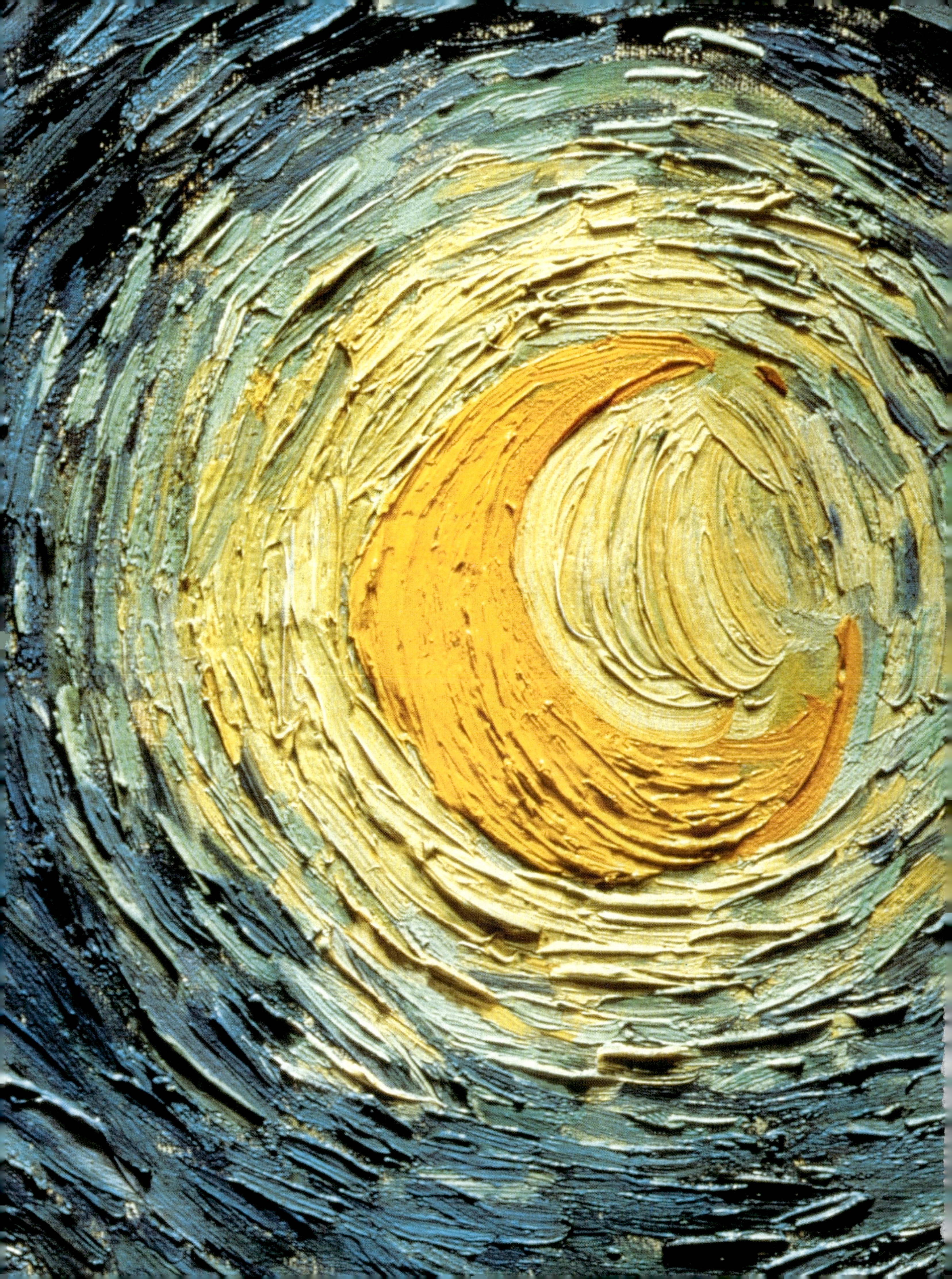

ANALYSIS OF THE WORK

THE NOCTURNAL LANDSCAPES

Van Gogh was not new to the nocturnal landscape: in 1888, still in Arles, he had painted *Starry Night over the Rhone*, in which he had explored the effect of starlight and of city lights combined with their reflection on the water. As he explained to his colleague Emile Bernard, in painting a starry night his intention was to see how the power of the imagination could exalt a view.

● Van Gogh wanted to transfigure spontaneous feeling before nature. "We can succeed in creating a more stirring, more pleasing nature than that which we can make out through a fleeting glance at reality."

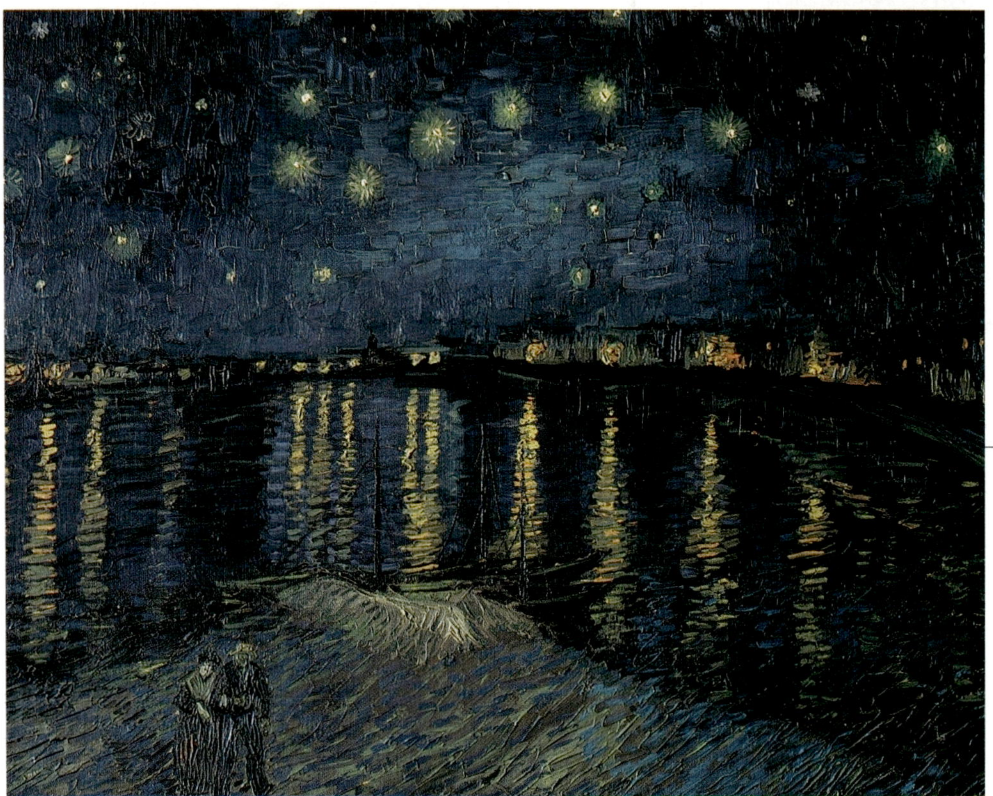

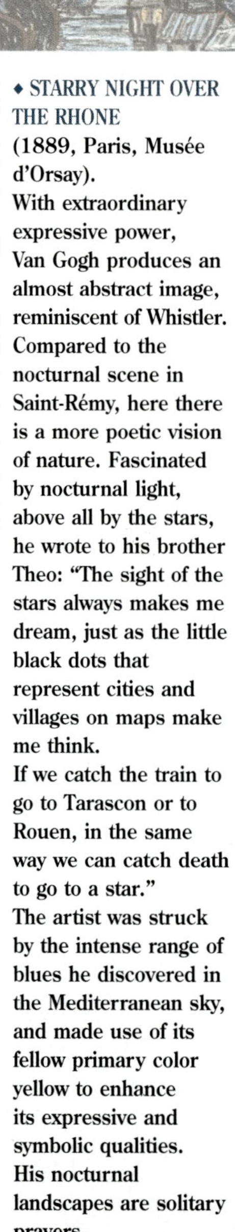

◆ STARRY NIGHT OVER THE RHONE
(1889, Paris, Musée d'Orsay).
With extraordinary expressive power, Van Gogh produces an almost abstract image, reminiscent of Whistler. Compared to the nocturnal scene in Saint-Rémy, here there is a more poetic vision of nature. Fascinated by nocturnal light, above all by the stars, he wrote to his brother Theo: "The sight of the stars always makes me dream, just as the little black dots that represent cities and villages on maps make me think.
If we catch the train to go to Tarascon or to Rouen, in the same way we can catch death to go to a star."
The artist was struck by the intense range of blues he discovered in the Mediterranean sky, and made use of its fellow primary color yellow to enhance its expressive and symbolic qualities.
His nocturnal landscapes are solitary prayers.

● The landscape thus takes the form of distorted outlines, with a dramatic tension in the lines. A feeling of a religious nature thus emerges from the convulsive vortexes of the sky, from the cypresses, which prefigure death, and from the disappearance of the human dimension in the immensity of nature, in a world pervaded by unreal lights. Through his art Van Gogh sought to console man for his misery; with a panic sentiment, but also with anger, he dreamt of returning to the bosom of nature.

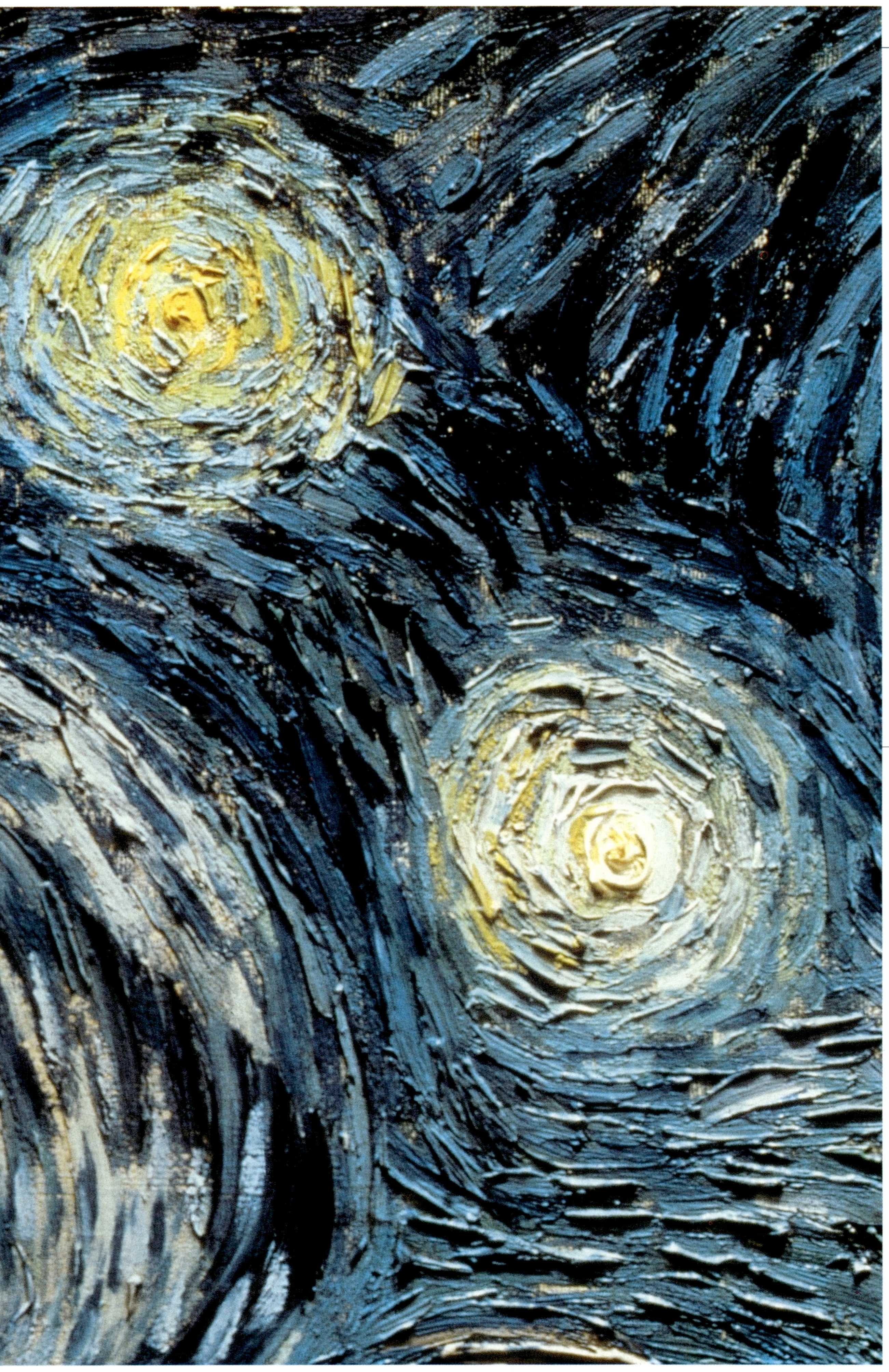

◆ FIERY STARS
The undulant movement that pervades the painting is a sort of vortex of nature, a dynamism that reminds us of the circularity of the universe.
The development of sidereal astronomy, that is the study of the stars, took place exactly at this time, a result of the discoveries of F.W. Herschel (1738-1822). Until then the stars had been considered as incandescent spheres. Herschel, observing the skies with large reflecting telescopes, discovered the planet Uranus and around 2,000 nebula, and also examined the apparent distribution of the stars above the celestial sphere, arriving at the first theories about the form of the sidereal universe.
It was towards the mid-nineteenth century, however, that the greatest advances in the field were made. Astronomers discovered the chemical nature of the substances contained in the atmosphere, their temperature, and the radial velocity of the stars.
Towards the end of the nineteenth century, photography came to the aid of astronomy: thanks in particular to the work of E.C. Pickering (1846-1919), modern stellar photometry was born. It is against this background of ferment and discovery that Van Gogh's interest in the stars should be seen.

STYLISTIC REFERENCES

Compared to his previous work, the canvases produced in Saint-Rémy display an undulating dynamism that is accompanied increasingly by a simplification of the compositive structure. A vertical thrust balances the paintings almost as if to express the efforts of man to reach the sky, a "stretching the hand towards the stars". The move towards a more essential pictorial style was also due to the artist's desire to explore the Synthetic style introduced by his friends Gauguin and Bernard, and the developments of Art Nouveau.

● However, although it reworks the forms of Art Nouveau, Van Gogh's arabesque does not have the same ornamental character. The simplification of the shapes and the syncopated rhythm of the brush-strokes are instruments of integration with the world; the lines are twisted and knotty, and give the movement a sense of instability and agitation.

● In these spirals and brush-strokes that curl around themselves, there is a break with traditional form that leads the artist to come close to abstraction. However, the exasperation of the brush-stroke does not result in the symbolism that Aurier found in it, but seems to be pervaded with a panic spirituality, an evocative transcendence learned from Millet.

● The painting also shows the evident influence of Japanese prints, which Van Gogh had been collecting for years. In Arles, he wrote that he had found a luminosity and an atmosphere that seemed similar to the idea he had formed of the East; "Here I am in Japan." He was fascinated by the incisive force of that unusual, lyrical art, which transfigured the visible and eliminated all descriptive intent, managing at the same time to maintain expressive immediacy.

◆ VAN GOGH'S WAVE
The wave crosses the starry sky like an unknown force that spreads until it involves the landscape, where the spiral movement returns. Van Gogh conveys through his imagination the anticipation of a cosmic event, and also of a personal event. The two-dimensional style learnt from Art Nouveau, also present in other works from this period, becomes in this case a fundamental element of the whole.

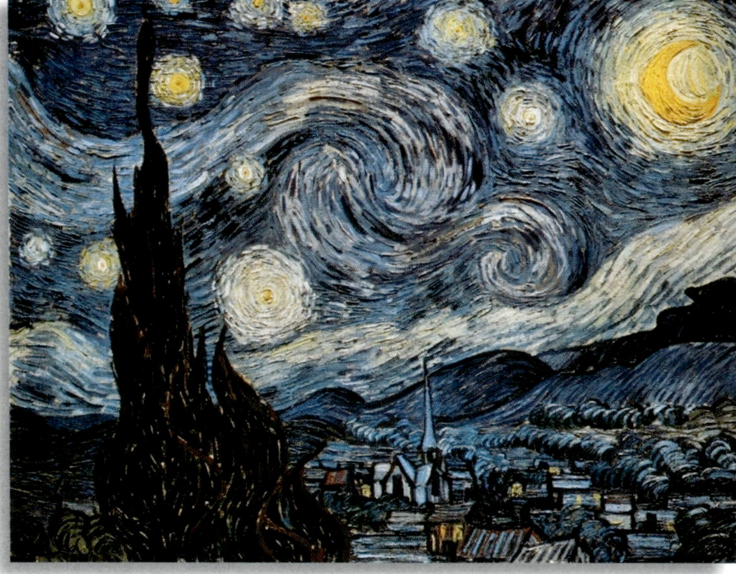

◆ VASES IN GALLÉ GLASS
The turn of the century saw the development of Art Nouveau, a style that aimed to restore an esthetic character to industrially produced objects. It confirmed the triumph of ornament to the detriment of structure; the volumes are reduced to an arabesque which, in its naturalistic motifs, often assumes a metamorphic character.

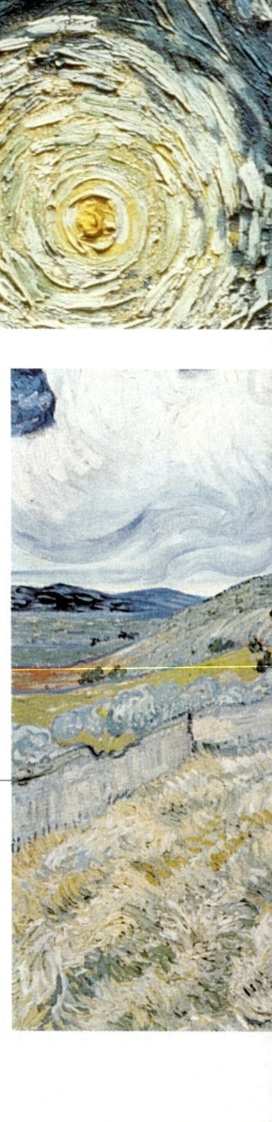

◆ WHEAT FIELD WITH LARGE CLOUD
(1889, Copenhagen, Ny Carlsberg Glyptotek). The diagonal line that crosses the painting reproduces the compositive structure of *Starry Night*. Here, however, the field is occupied mainly by the land and the undulating movement of the ears of wheat. The realism is contradicted once again by the two-dimensional arabesques of the sky.

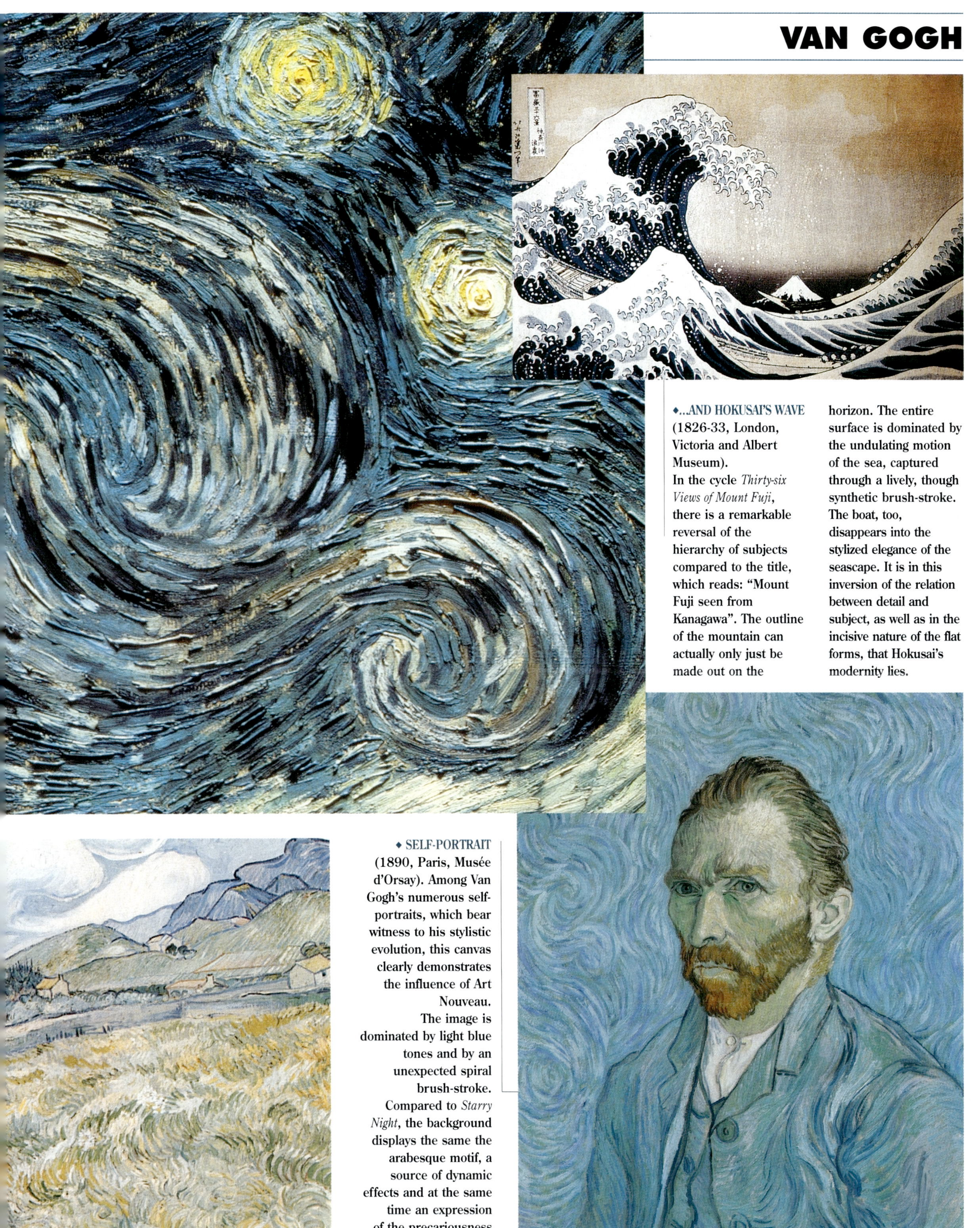

◆ ...AND HOKUSAI'S WAVE (1826-33, London, Victoria and Albert Museum). In the cycle *Thirty-six Views of Mount Fuji*, there is a remarkable reversal of the hierarchy of subjects compared to the title, which reads: "Mount Fuji seen from Kanagawa". The outline of the mountain can actually only just be made out on the horizon. The entire surface is dominated by the undulating motion of the sea, captured through a lively, though synthetic brush-stroke. The boat, too, disappears into the stylized elegance of the seascape. It is in this inversion of the relation between detail and subject, as well as in the incisive nature of the flat forms, that Hokusai's modernity lies.

◆ SELF-PORTRAIT (1890, Paris, Musée d'Orsay). Among Van Gogh's numerous self-portraits, which bear witness to his stylistic evolution, this canvas clearly demonstrates the influence of Art Nouveau. The image is dominated by light blue tones and by an unexpected spiral brush-stroke. Compared to *Starry Night*, the background displays the same the arabesque motif, a source of dynamic effects and at the same time an expression of the precariousness of life.

INSANITY AND EMARGINATION

MAISON DE SANTÉ
DE
SAINT-REMY DE PROVENCE
(BOUCHES-DU-RHÔNE.)
ÉTABLISSEMENT PRIVÉ
CONSACRÉ AU TRAITEMENT DES ALIÉNÉS DES DEUX SEXES.

In order to understand the work of Van Gogh, we first have to strip his figure of all the elements attributed to him by popular mythology over the years, turning him into the legend of the mad genius, the artist as a misunderstood prophet. Driven by the various analyses of the critics and the ingenuousness of the public, an image has been created of a man "with the soul of a visionary" (Aurier), an image that must be discredited.

● The two episodes of self-inflicted injury, cutting off part of his ear and shooting himself, have fed the legend and finally created a character to which even the cinema has repeatedly chosen to pay homage. From Irving Stone's 1934 romanticized *Lust for Life* to Vincent Minelli's equally sentimental 1956 version, with Kirk Douglas in the lead role, Van Gogh has been forced into the romantic role of the emarginated artist or the genius inspired by his own insanity.

● The pathological side of his existence, which dominated his private life, should be kept well apart from the interpretation of his artistic output. The anxiety that transpires from his works seems to be the result of emargination rather than of madness. Van Gogh represents the tragedy of a man destined to remain misunderstood, and therefore rejected, by society.

● Van Gogh's doctors spoke of epilepsy, and this diagnosis is still generally accepted as the explanation for his problems. And yet his life had a difficult and tormented progress, characterized by professional and personal failures, which only took the form of mental illness in the last three years. The progress of his life was that of a social misfit suffering immensely from solitude, despite his spontaneous affection for other people. It is in this complex tangle of events that we should identify the roots of the tension that emerges in his paintings.

● In his letters Van Gogh describes his unhappiness with great self-awareness, aiming to fight it through art, which for him meant panic involvement in nature rather than a moment of creative *raptus*. It would be difficult otherwise to explain the extreme lucidity of an artist who describes the genesis of his paintings, his models and his artistic research with such critical acumen.

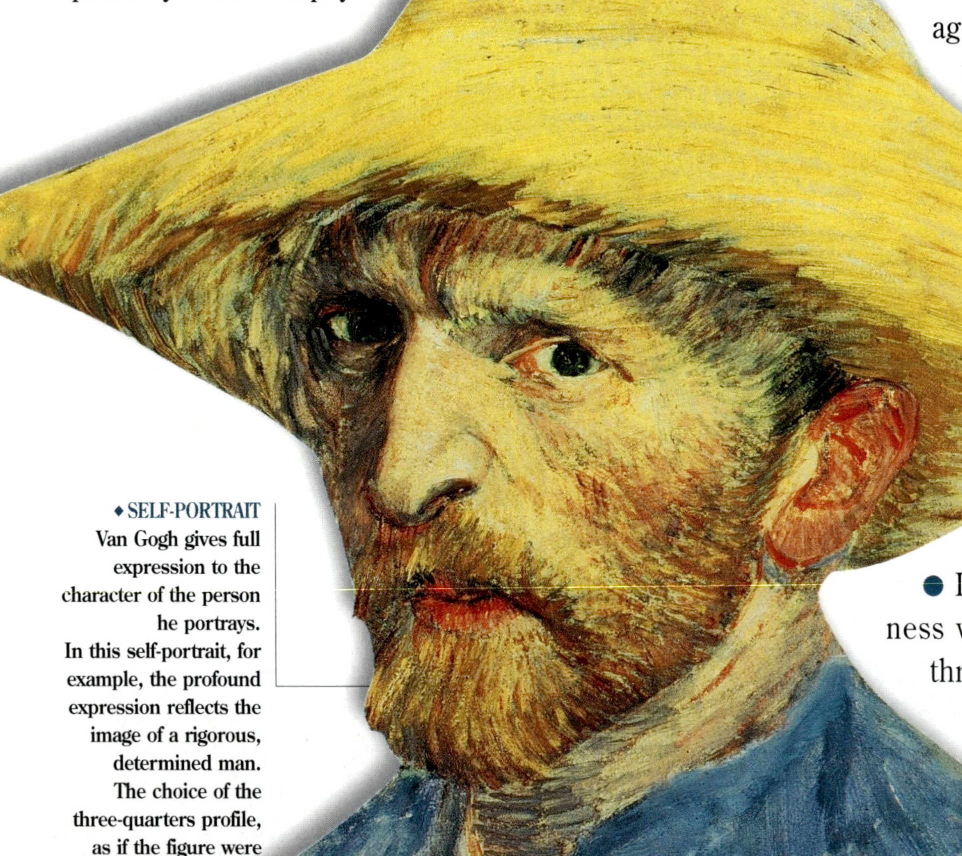

◆ SELF-PORTRAIT
Van Gogh gives full expression to the character of the person he portrays. In this self-portrait, for example, the profound expression reflects the image of a rigorous, determined man. The choice of the three-quarters profile, as if the figure were about to turn round, reveals the artist's restless soul.

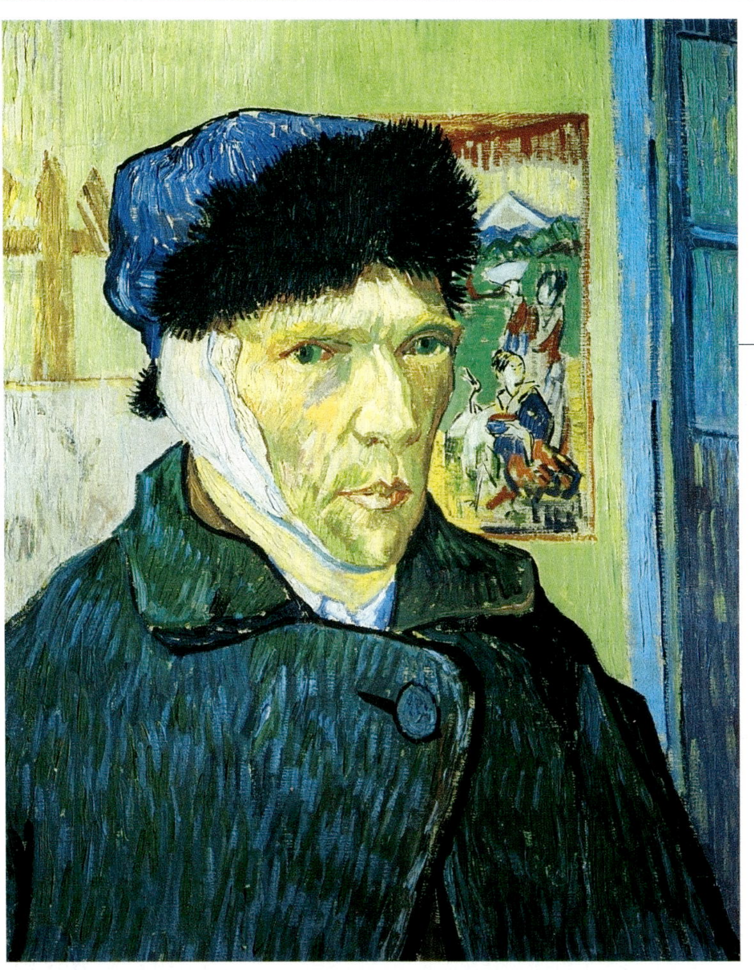

◆ SELF-PORTRAIT WITH BANDAGED EAR (1889, London, Courtauld Institute Galleries). In December 1888, in a fit of anger after an argument with Gauguin, Van Gogh cut off part of his left ear and gave it to a prostitute from Arles. This work was painted one month after the event, and reveals the discomfort of the artist, who depicts himself at home, in front of his easel and his beloved Japanese prints, but wearing a hat, like a passing stranger.

◆ THE GARDEN OF THE HOSPITAL IN ARLES (1889, Winterthur, private collection). After his self-inflicted injury, Van Gogh was locked up in the hospital in Arles. The gradual improvement of his physical and mental condition allowed him to resume painting and to distract himself from his solitude. He made a number of sketches of the courtyard of the hospital, the only subject that could instill in him a sense of peace and of temporary relief. Compared to the white of the asylum, the colors of the flowers and the intensity of the light of the sun acquire an evocative, nostalgic power expressed with surprising efficacy.

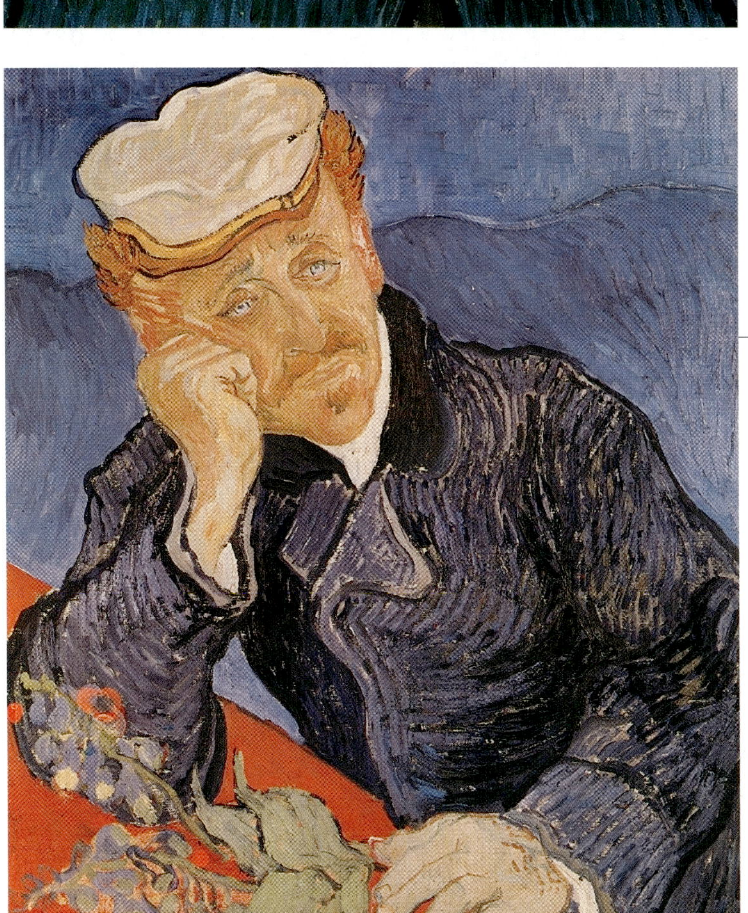

◆PORTRAIT OF DOCTOR GACHET (1890, Paris, Musée d'Orsay). Van Gogh spent his final, tormented days at the home of the doctor, a passionate collector and friend of many Parisian artists. In the portrait, of great introspective power, the doctor has a disconsolate expression, reflected in the diagonal composition of the painting.

◆ CORRIDOR IN THE SAINT-PAUL ASYLUM (1889, New York, Museum of Modern Art). Van Gogh depicts the desolate corridors of the asylum (left). This is the environment in which Van Gogh's drama unfolded: he was forced to live together with patients who had serious mental illnesses. His solitude and the fact that it was impossible to escape caused him great suffering.

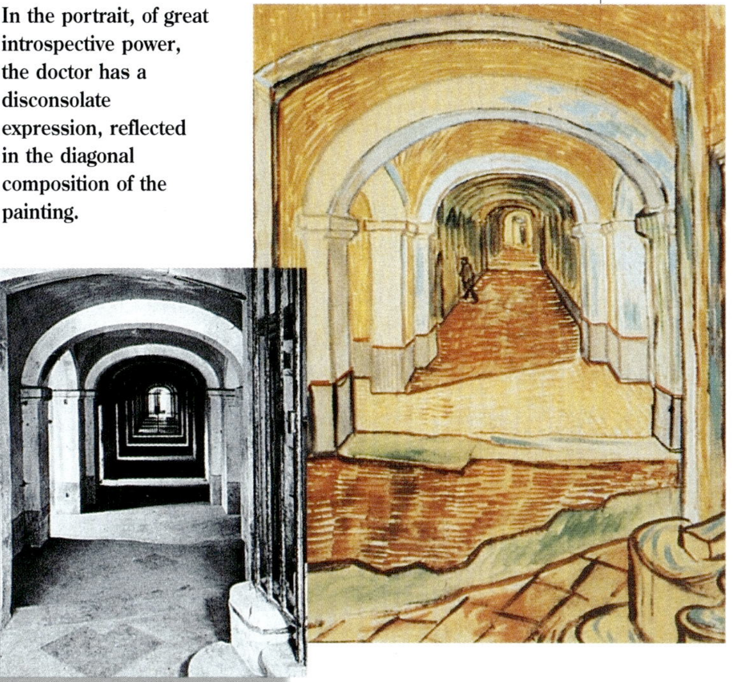

THE CONQUEST OF COLOR

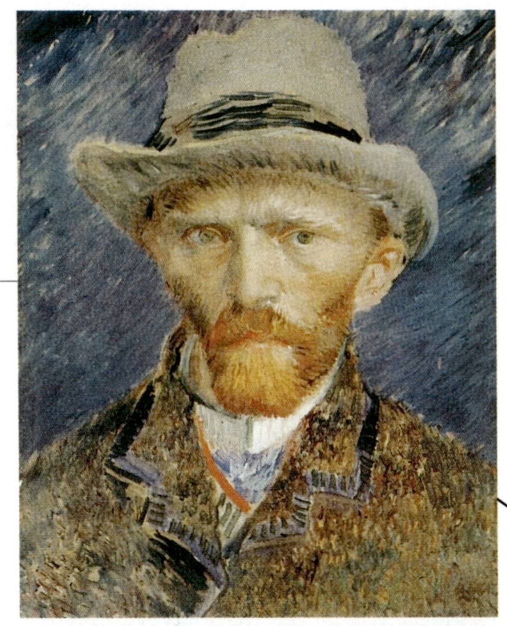

◆ SELF-PORTRAIT WITH GREY FELT HAT (1887, Amsterdam, Stedelijk Museum). Compared to the previous works of his Dutch period, the painting presents a curious contradiction. Van Gogh had always expressed his desire to live like humble people, but here he depicts himself with a fine suit and a confident expression, far from the suffering of peasants ands miners. Here he introduces the broken lines of the neo-Impressionist style.

At the outset of his career as a painter, Van Gogh was mainly influenced by the Dutch realist school, by Rembrandt, Hals and Rubens, from whom he borrowed the use of chiaroscuro and the dramatic contrasts of light and shadow. Their dark tones reflected the misery and the fatigue of humble subjects. The long, aggressive brush-strokes emphasize the harshness of the features and the tormented outlines.

● In 1886, Van Gogh went to Paris, where he discovered Impressionism. Attracted by the chromatic power and the intuitions of a form of art that flowed from the artist's emotions, he read the writings of Charles Blanc and studied the scientific theories that lay behind Impressionism, in particular the theories about the complementary juxtaposition of colors. During his two years in Paris his lines became more fluid, while his palette lightened and yielded to the attraction of colors. His brush-stroke became shorter in the Divisionist touches learnt from Seurat, and in the streaks of bright, lumpy color for which he is famous.

● His flight to Provence coincided with his discovery of light. There was now an unexpected brio in his canvases, the result of the warm, lively palette. Color was no longer only a transcription of form, but became an autonomous expression, "a means of bringing out character". The rhythmic brush-strokes exalted the energy of the gesture, allowing the artist to conquer reality and to become aware of his own essence. Through a style full of emotional tension, Van Gogh produced an indissoluble link between art and life.

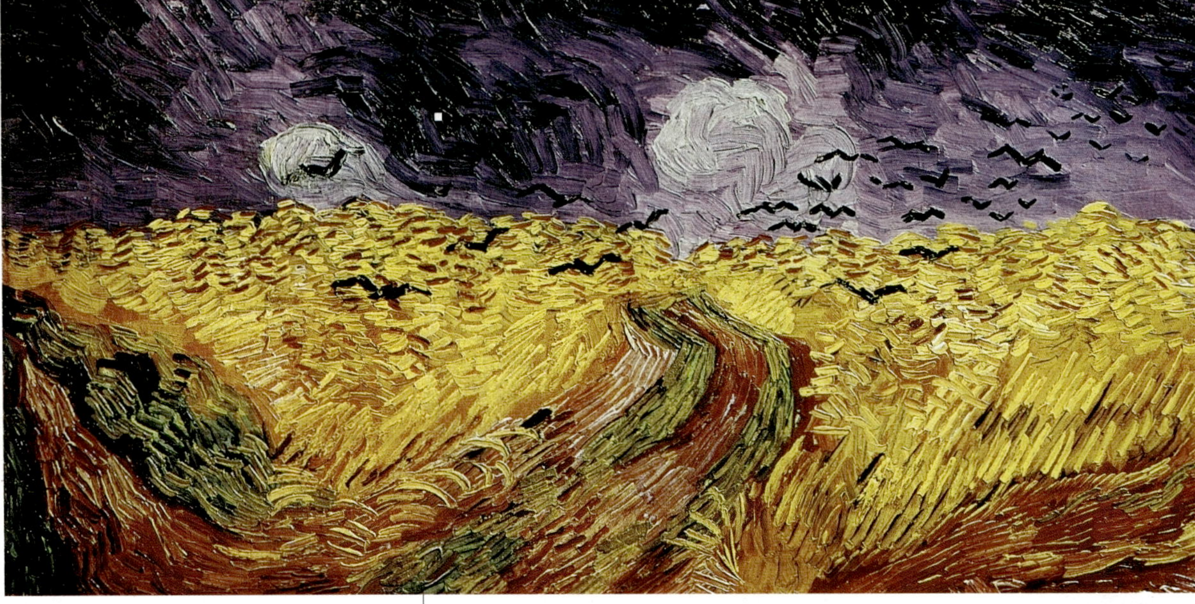

◆ WHEAT FIELD WITH CROWS (1890, Amsterdam, Rijksmuseum Vincent Van Gogh). The work is one of the last produced by the painter before his death, during the three months in which he lived in Auvers, and is consequently considered as his pictorial testament. With untidy, energetic movements, and using a flat brush, he traces rough lines on the canvas, like stormy currents crossing the earth and the sky.

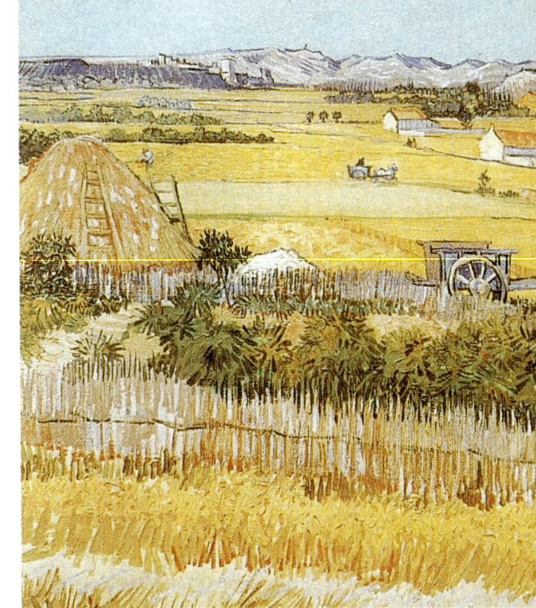

◆ FARMHOUSES
(1883, Amsterdam, Rijksmuseum Vincent Van Gogh). During this period Van Gogh's work is characterized by a somber palette and subdued colors. The landscapes are devoid of sources of light. The lack of any human figures to enliven the scene throws a veil of desolation over the farm.

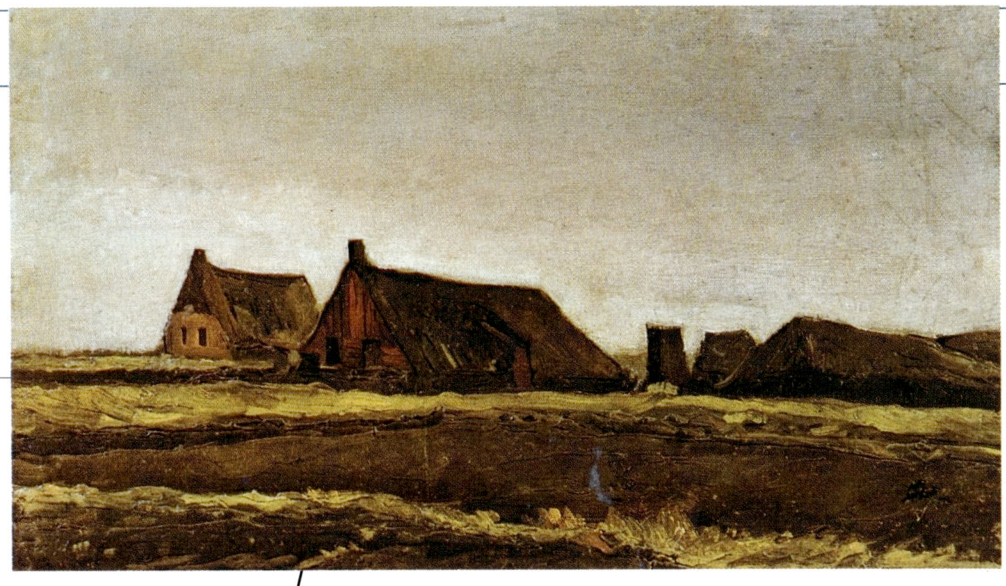

◆ WEAVER, SEEN FROM THE FRONT
(1884, Otterlo, Rijksmuseum Kröller-Müller).
The painting is typical of Van Gogh's early production, when his attention is concentrated on portraing workers toiling bravely or resting, often near to collapse.
The imposing frame of the loom swallows up the human subject.

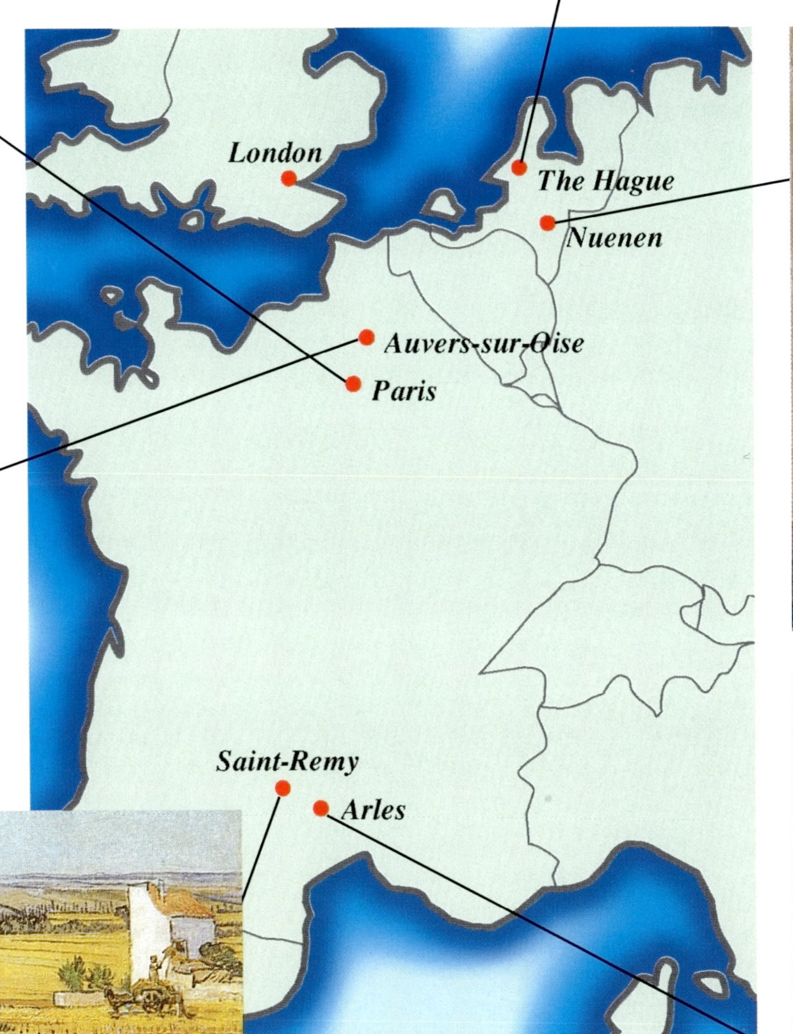

◆ HARVEST AT LA CRAU, WITH MONTMAJOUR IN THE BACKGROUND
(1888, Amsterdam, Rijksmuseum Vincent Van Gogh). The sun-drenched landscapes of Provence filled Van Gogh with a new sense of enthusiasm. "Nature in the South," he wrote, "cannot be portrayed with the palette of the North. My palette is now full of colors. By reinforcing them one reacquires serenity and harmony."

◆ L'ARLESIENNE (MADAME GINOUX)
(1890, Otterlo, Rijksmuseum Kröller-Müller).
The image represents M.me Ginoux, who Van Gogh painted several times, also in the company of Gauguin.
She was one of the few people willing to be portrayed by the artist, unconcerned by the prejudices that had grown up as a result of his eccentricity.

PRODUCTION: TECHNIQUE

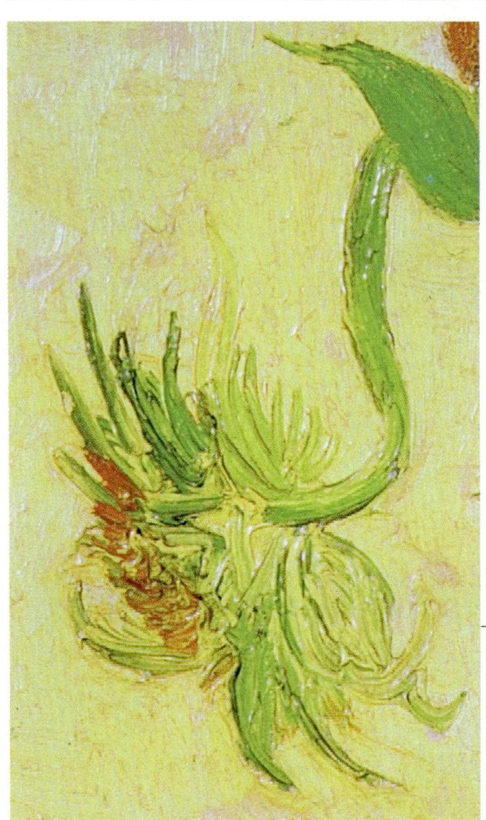

◆ A COLD HEART
The blue heart of the sunflower is the only example of cold tones, and by contrast exalts the warm character of the yellow. The thick layer of color animates the canvas, like those of other flowers.

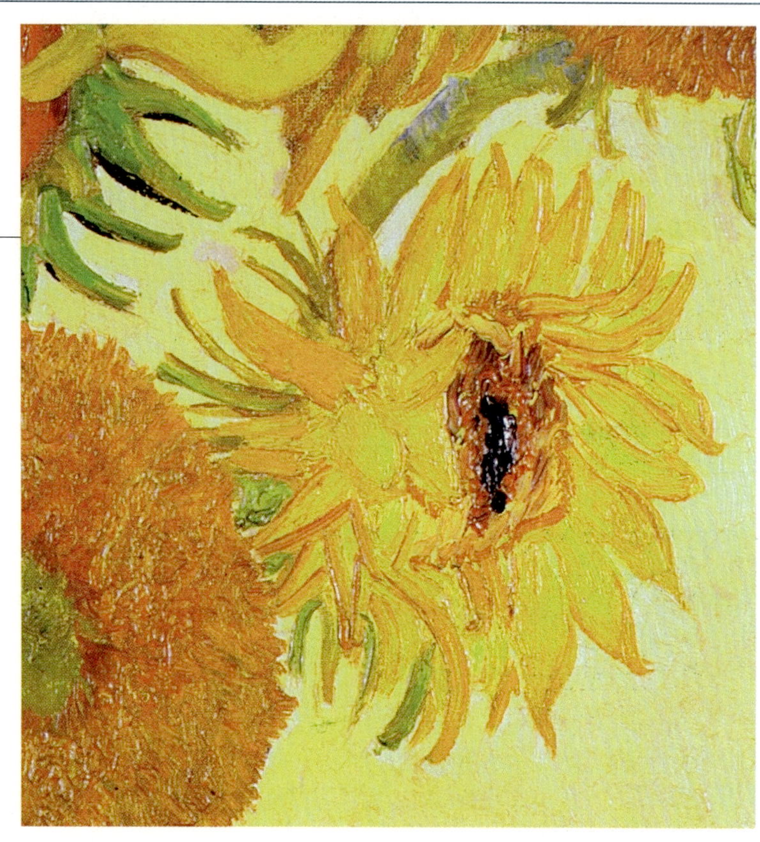

◆ THE BENT SUNFLOWER
Although the image is a hymn to life, it does contain a note of melancholy. Beauty and serenity are recognized as ephemeral graces. It is the bent sunflower, no longer able to hold itself up, that conveys this memento mori.

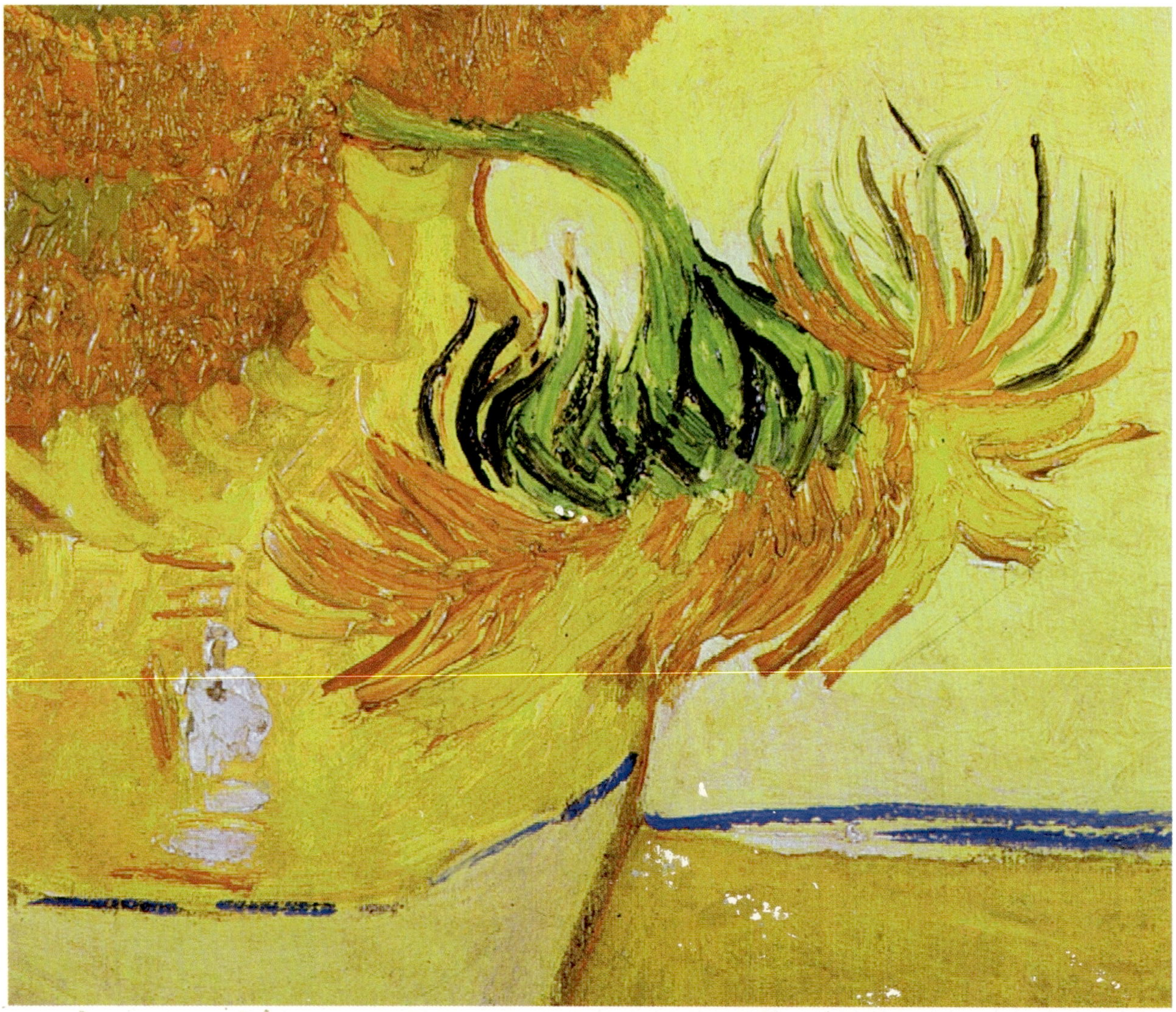

◆ VASE WITH SUNFLOWERS
(1889, Amsterdam, Rijksmuseum Vincent Van Gogh). No still life had ever been as explosive as this! In Arles Van Gogh discovered light and the almost dazzling yellow of the wheat fields and the sunflowers. And so the gloomy atmosphere of Holland, and the disorderly vivacity of the Parisian works, are overturned in a sudden blaze of color. In the twelve canvases devoted to this subject, the color yellow dominates with its euphoric, sunny power, which overflows into all the other colors. The color yellow also has symbolic value, alluding to the light and the presence of the divine.

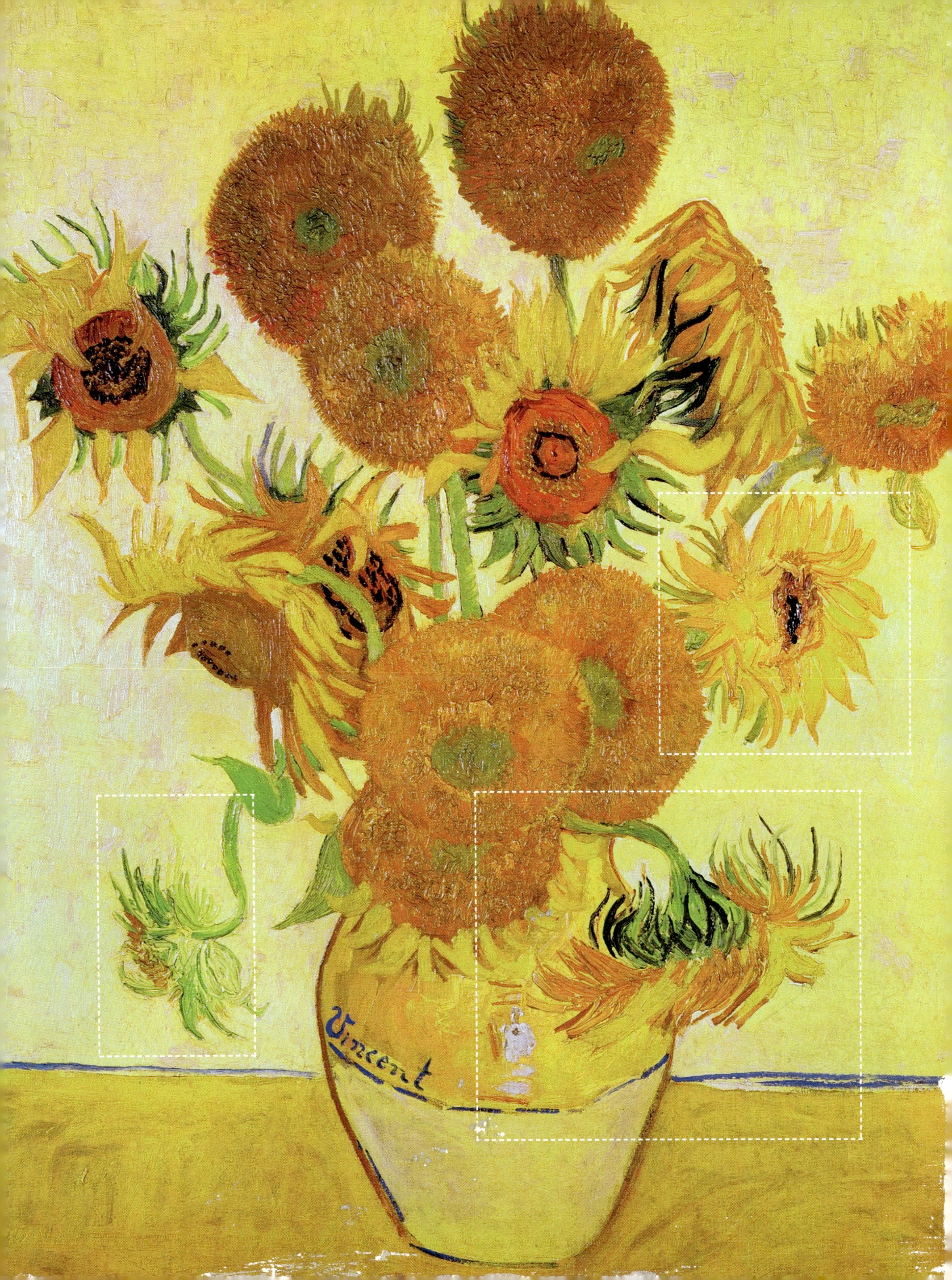
Vincent

DEFORMED PERSPECTIVE

In the paintings produced in Holland, Van Gogh applied the methods of perspective learned from the Dutch masters of the seventeenth century. In Paris, his contacts with the Impressionists and the neo-Impressionists, as well as his discovery of Japanese prints, brought about a gradual abandonment of profundity, and of the conception of the painting as a window.

●Space was increasingly conceived of as the expression of a subjective interpretation of reality. This is why he painted objects with flat colors and sometimes exaggerated the proportions, or altered them to create a state of tension.

●He generally preferred to adopt a very high point of view with respect to the line of the horizon, a choice that emphasized the immensity of nature compared to the human figures. In this way he conveyed an effect of disorientation, echoed by the choice of colors, which seem to create a slight oscillation in the objects.

●Continuing to simplify the composition, in his last works Van Gogh depicted landscapes in which the relations between near and far, or between large and small, are indistinguishable. The objects lose all trace of stability and are twisted into elongated, writhing shapes, like the cypresses that resemble tongues of fire. Everything is absorbed into a mess of color and a confused perspective.

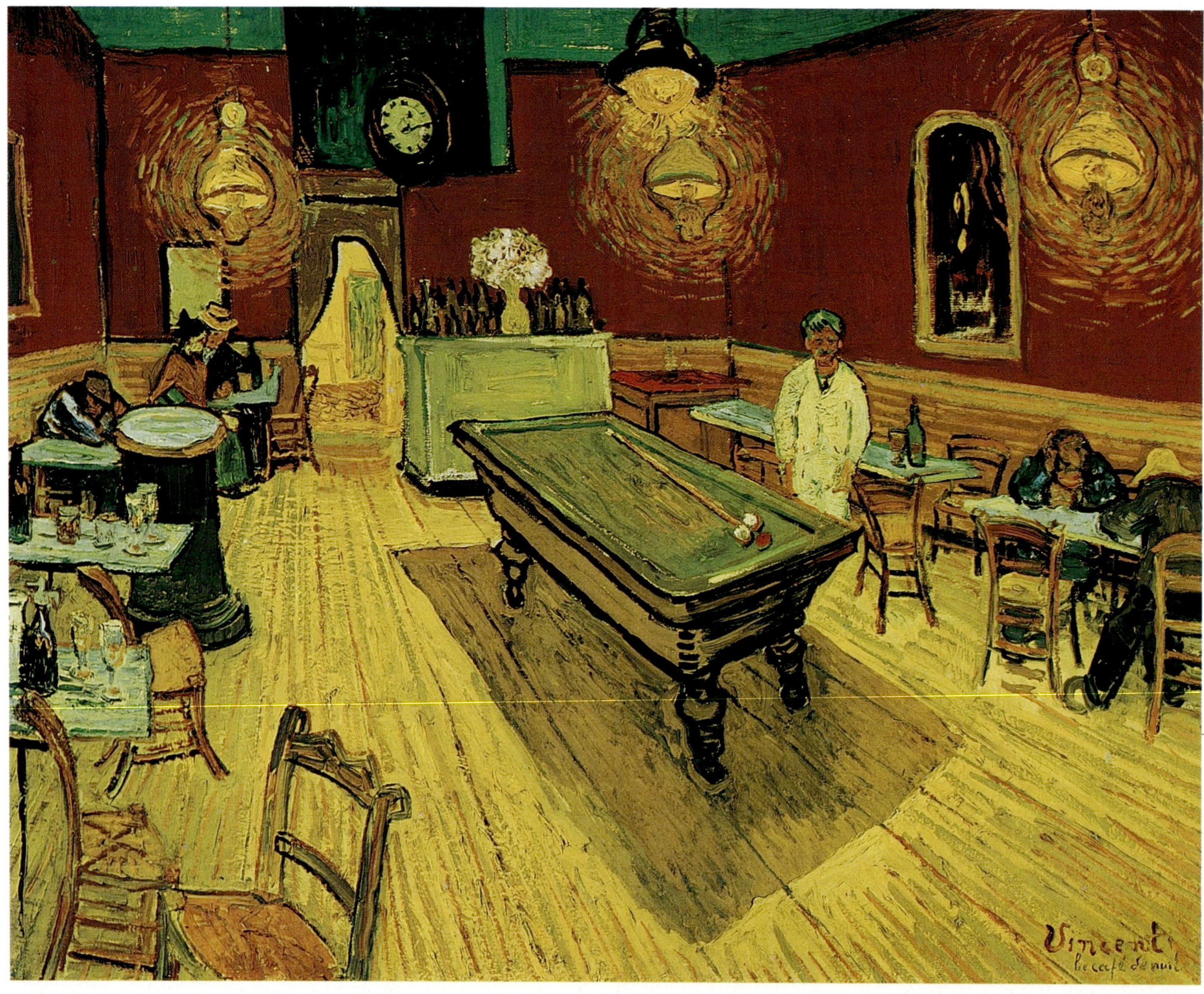

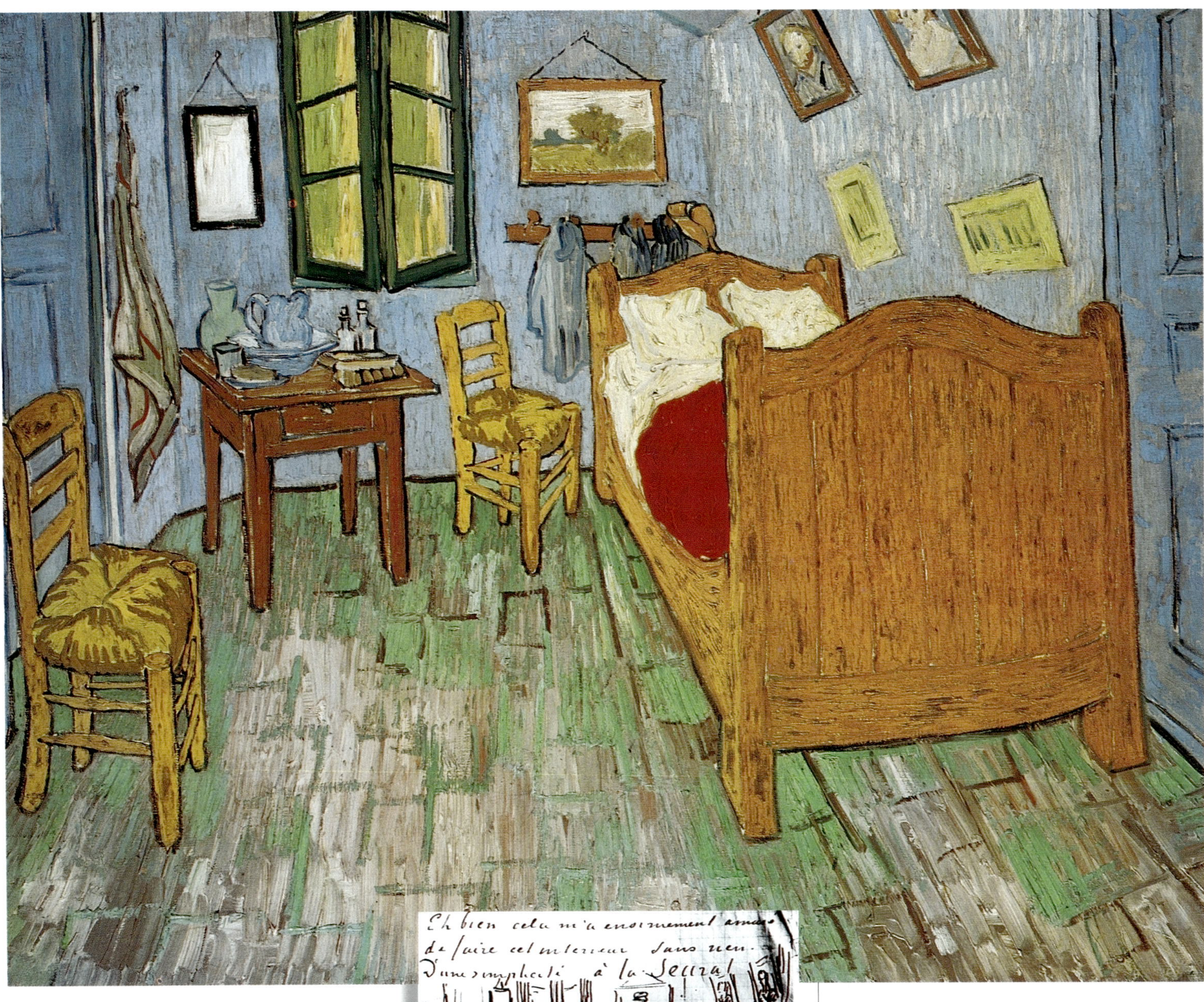

THE NIGHT CAFE IN THE PLACE LAMARTINE IN ARLES
(1888, New Haven, Yale University Art Gallery).
At the beginning of his stay in Arles, Van Gogh often went to this cafe to find company or relief. "In my painting *The Cafe Terrace* I tried to make it clear that a cafe is a place where one can come to ruin, go mad, or commit crimes. I tried to express the tenebrous power of a tavern." Through these words the artist illustrates the criteria of his formal interpretation.
The figures are captured in their solitude, lost in an environment they cannot even embrace with their eyes.
The perspective indicated by the floor has a high line of horizon and seems to be dominated by the billiard table.
There are, however, further lines of flight such as those of the walls, which disturb the unity of the composition.
Thus the image appears unstable and disconnected, as is also evident in the chairs in the foreground.

Eh bien cela m'a énormément amusé de faire cet intérieur sans rien. D'une simplicité à la Seurat;

A teintes plates mais grossièrement brossées en pleine pâte les murs lilas pâle le sol d'un rouge rompu et fané les chaises et le lit jaune de chrome les oreillers et le drap citron vert très pâle la couverture rouge sang la table à toilette orangée la cuvette bleue la fenêtre verte J'avais voulu exprimer un repos absolu par tous ces tons très divers vous voyez et où il n'y a de blanc que la petite note que donne le miroir à cadre noir (pour fourrer encore la quatrième paire de complémentaires dedans) Enfin vous verrez cela avec les autres et nous en causerons car je ne sais souvent

VINCENT'S BEDROOM IN ARLES
(1888, Amsterdam, Rijksmuseum Vincent Van Gogh).
From October 1888, Van Gogh put up his friend Gauguin in his room in Arles.
This subject, of which there are also later versions produced at the Saint-Rémy hospital, was executed shortly before Gauguin's arrival. This is clear in the fact that there are two of many of the objects: the water jugs, the pillows, the chairs, and the brushes.
On the wall is one of Van Gogh's many self-portraits, while his straw hat can also be seen behind the bed.
The painter wrote that: "I very much enjoyed doing this indoor scene with nothing, of a simplicity reminiscent of Seurat: with flat colors, applied coarsely without dissolving the paint. I wanted to express absolute rest."
Van Gogh adopts a realistic point of view and arranges the objects in apparent order.
And yet the inclination of the paintings and the juxtaposition of colors unsettle the balance of the canvas.

SELF-PORTRAITS

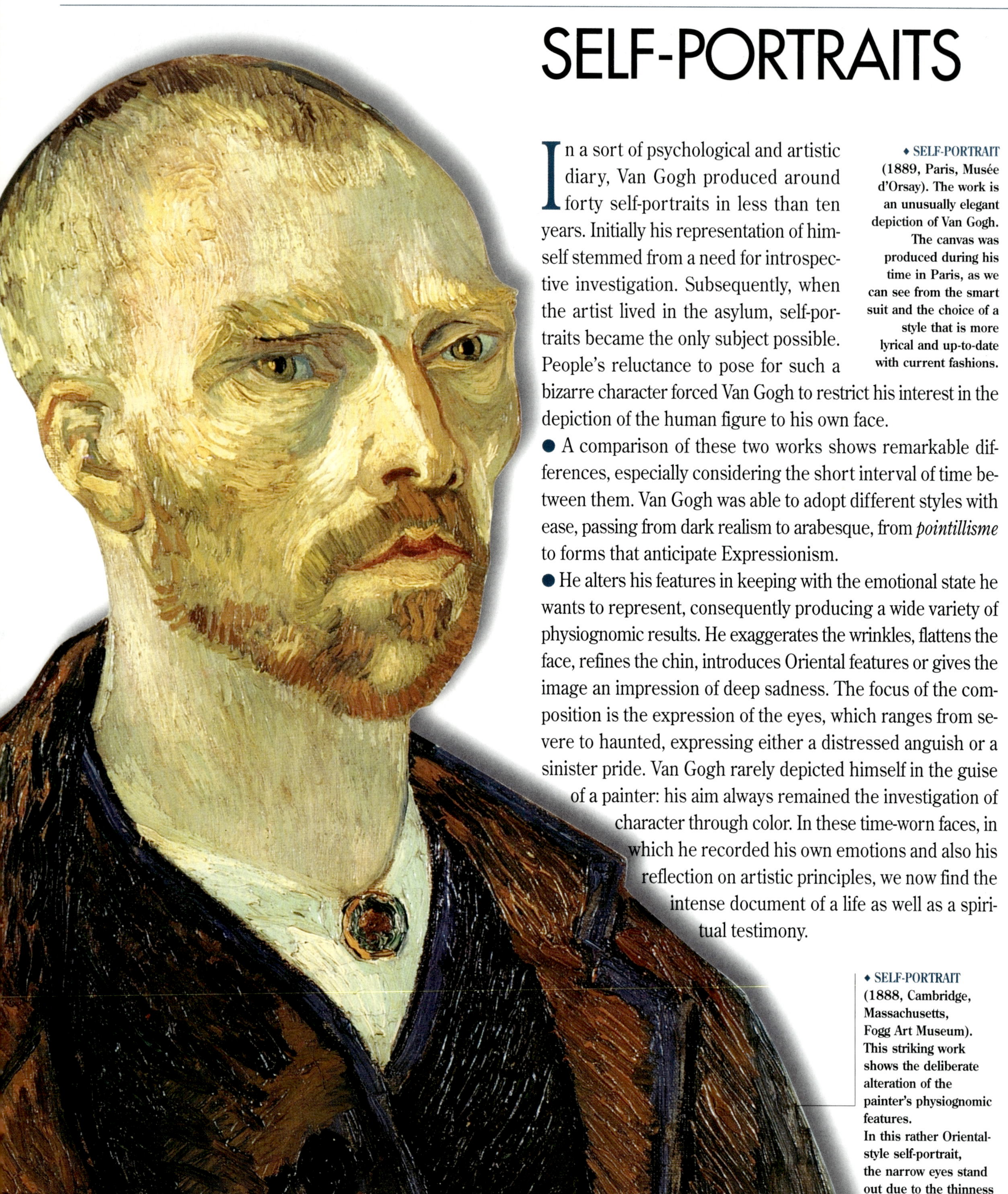

◆ SELF-PORTRAIT (1889, Paris, Musée d'Orsay). The work is an unusually elegant depiction of Van Gogh. The canvas was produced during his time in Paris, as we can see from the smart suit and the choice of a style that is more lyrical and up-to-date with current fashions.

In a sort of psychological and artistic diary, Van Gogh produced around forty self-portraits in less than ten years. Initially his representation of himself stemmed from a need for introspective investigation. Subsequently, when the artist lived in the asylum, self-portraits became the only subject possible. People's reluctance to pose for such a bizarre character forced Van Gogh to restrict his interest in the depiction of the human figure to his own face.

● A comparison of these two works shows remarkable differences, especially considering the short interval of time between them. Van Gogh was able to adopt different styles with ease, passing from dark realism to arabesque, from *pointillisme* to forms that anticipate Expressionism.

● He alters his features in keeping with the emotional state he wants to represent, consequently producing a wide variety of physiognomic results. He exaggerates the wrinkles, flattens the face, refines the chin, introduces Oriental features or gives the image an impression of deep sadness. The focus of the composition is the expression of the eyes, which ranges from severe to haunted, expressing either a distressed anguish or a sinister pride. Van Gogh rarely depicted himself in the guise of a painter: his aim always remained the investigation of character through color. In these time-worn faces, in which he recorded his own emotions and also his reflection on artistic principles, we now find the intense document of a life as well as a spiritual testimony.

◆ SELF-PORTRAIT (1888, Cambridge, Massachusetts, Fogg Art Museum). This striking work shows the deliberate alteration of the painter's physiognomic features. In this rather Oriental-style self-portrait, the narrow eyes stand out due to the thinness of the face.

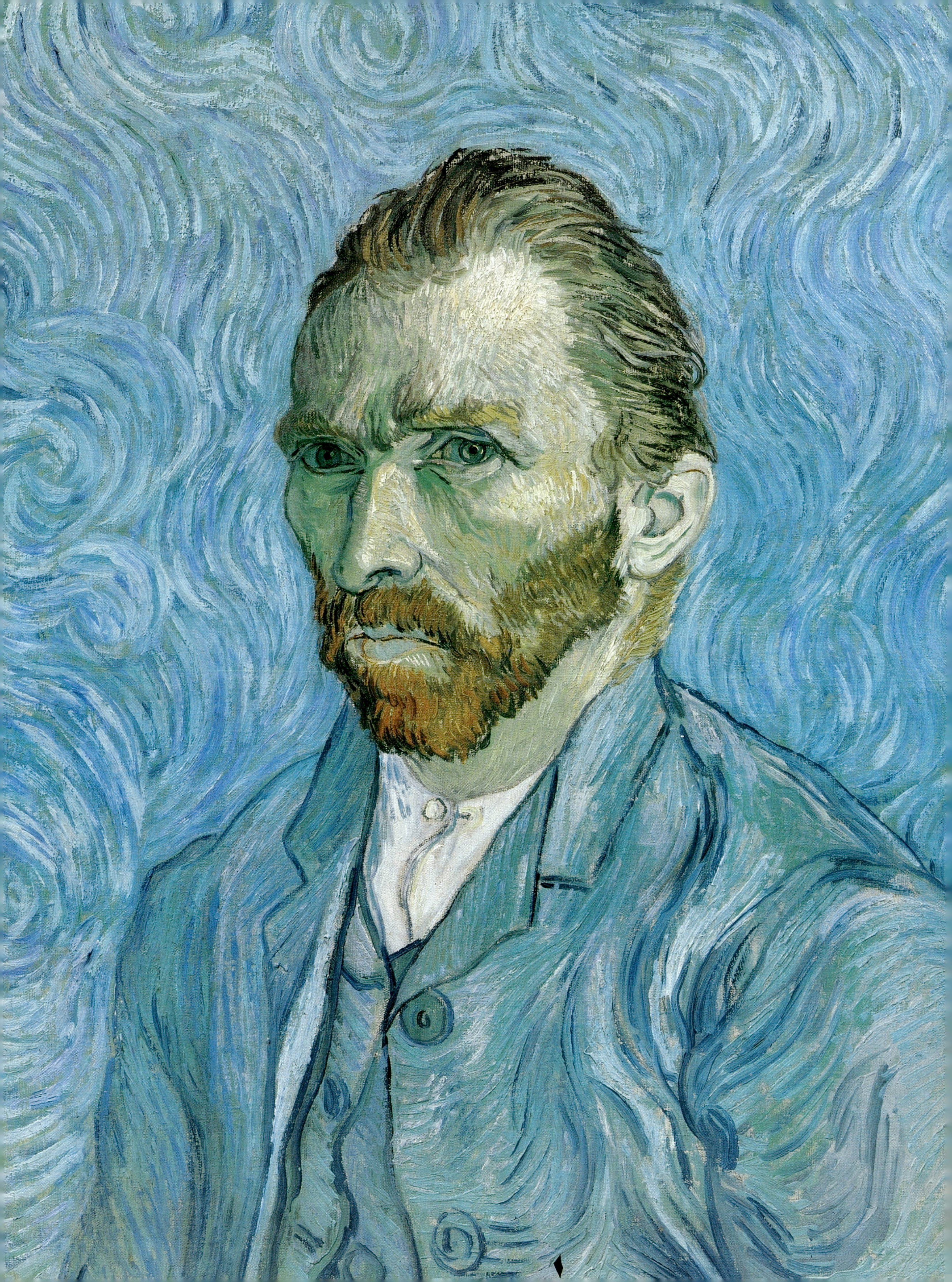

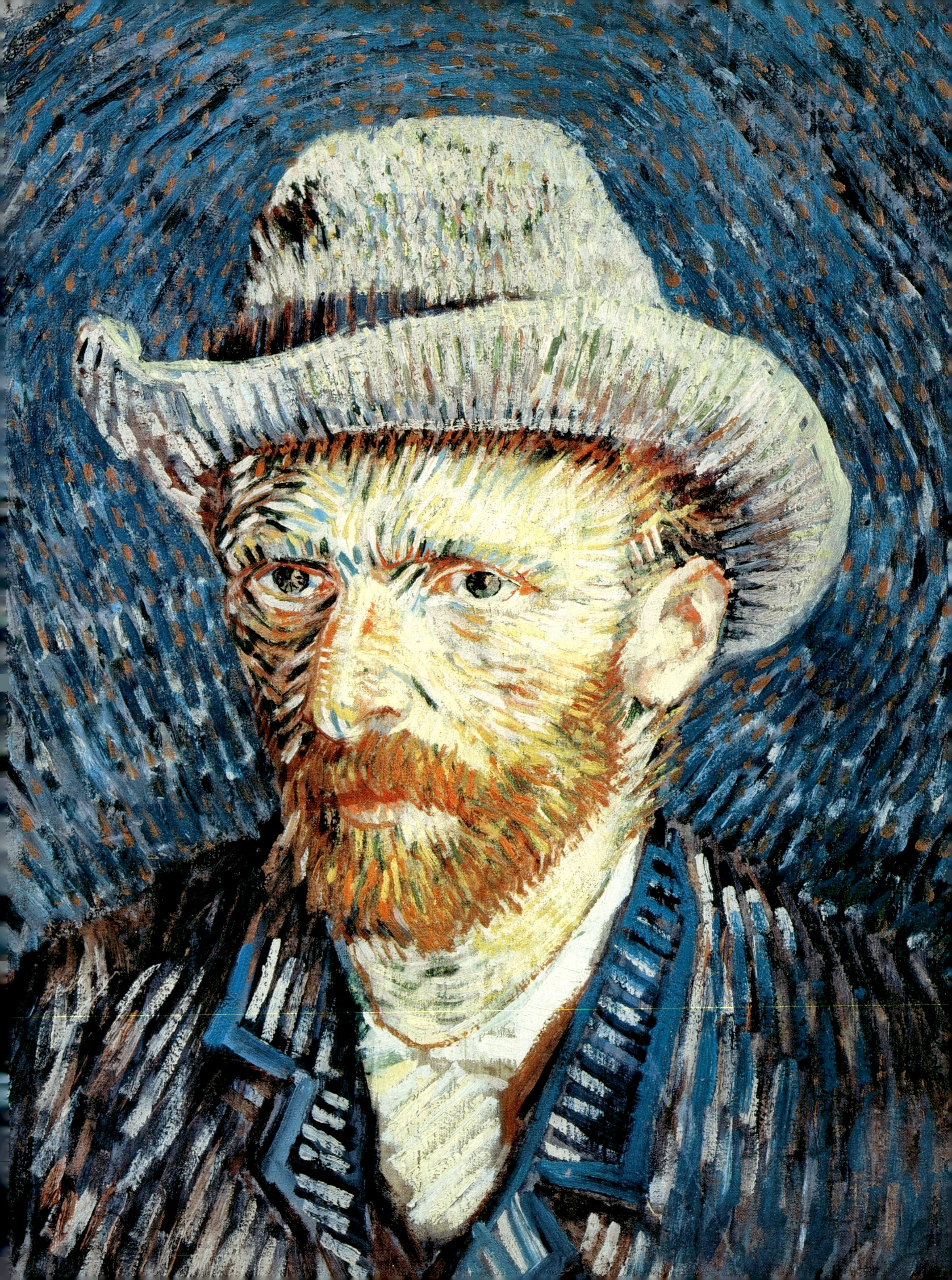

◆ SELF-PORTRAIT (1887, Amsterdam, Rijksmuseum Vincent Van Gogh). In this Parisian self-portrait Van Gogh attempts to follow the contemporary experiments of Divisionism and shortens his brush-stroke. His palette is enlivened with vibrant colors, conveying a sense of *joie de vivre*. In order to increase the dynamism of the subject, he plays with brush-strokes traced in a concentric rhythm, creating a sort of vortex around his own head.

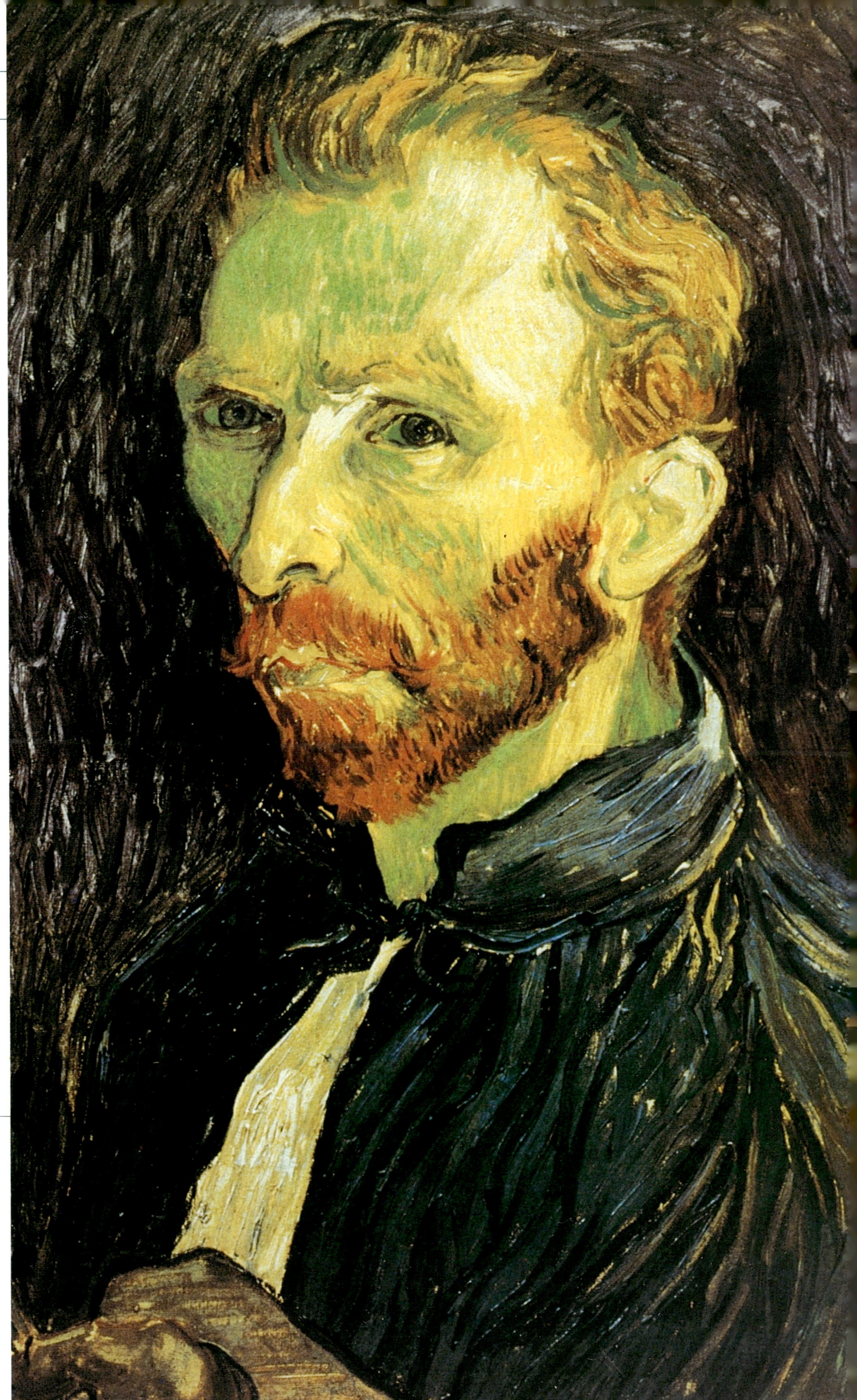

◆ SELF-PORTRAIT (1889, New York, Whitney Collection). Dressed as a painter, the artist expresses the fundamental relation between life and art: painting must save him from the temptation to yield to despair. The image was produced, in fact, during his stay in the hospital of Saint-Rémy, when self-portrait was the only alternative possible to making copies from prints of works by Millet. The choice of rather sour greenish tones, underlined by an unnatural light, gives the work a disturbing character.

HUMAN SUFFERING

Faithful to the seventeenth-century Dutch tradition, at the beginning of his career Van Gogh depicted scenes of humble workers. Their hardship inspired him with a sense of warm sympathy. Weavers, fishermen, peasants and miners dominate the drawings produced in the Hague and Nuenen. The tense poses, the dramatic chiaroscuro, and the tormented expressions bear witness to conditions of poverty and misery that contrast with the conventional well-being described by other painters.

● Critics have seen in Van Gogh a form of socialism similar to that which inspired Courbet and Millet. With his dual nature as "monk and painter", he aimed to console the workers through his sermons and his works, conferring a new dignity on their suffering. Right from the outset he was attracted by concrete reality, without trace of false embellishment. His paintings reek of "lard, smoke, potato steam". The theme of the poor did not stem from an artistic choice, but rather from a shared experience of everyday life.

● Van Gogh thus used dark, earthy colors, devoid of light, almost as if to underline the complete lack of hope. In the faces, the coarse features are rendered with rough, thick strokes, and their transcription onto the canvas assumes the form of a further aggression. Elsewhere, as in his drawings, the artist's interest is not with physiognomic features, which remain anonymous, but with the expression, in the form of vibrant emblems, of gestures of suffering or the fatigue of work.

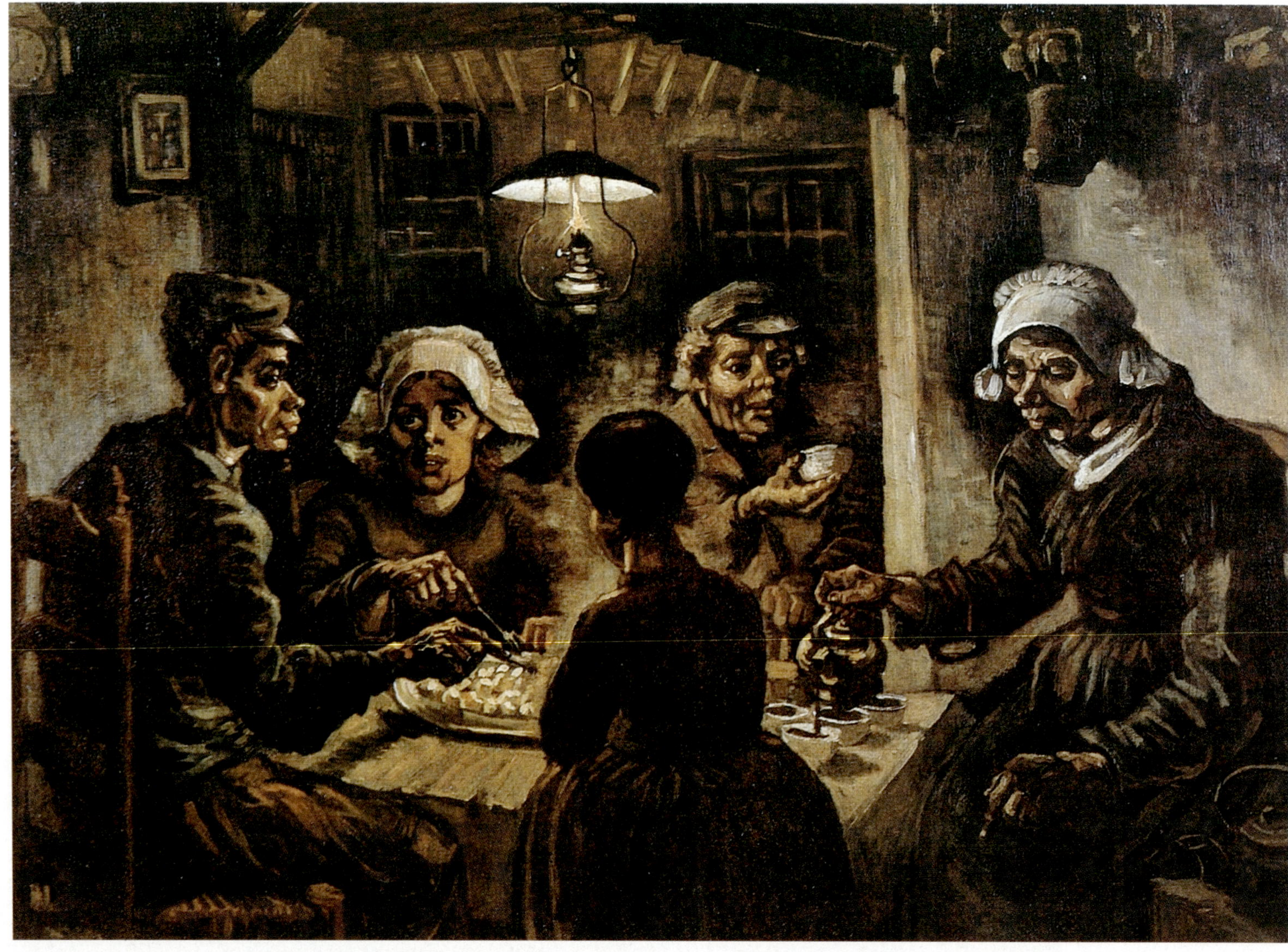

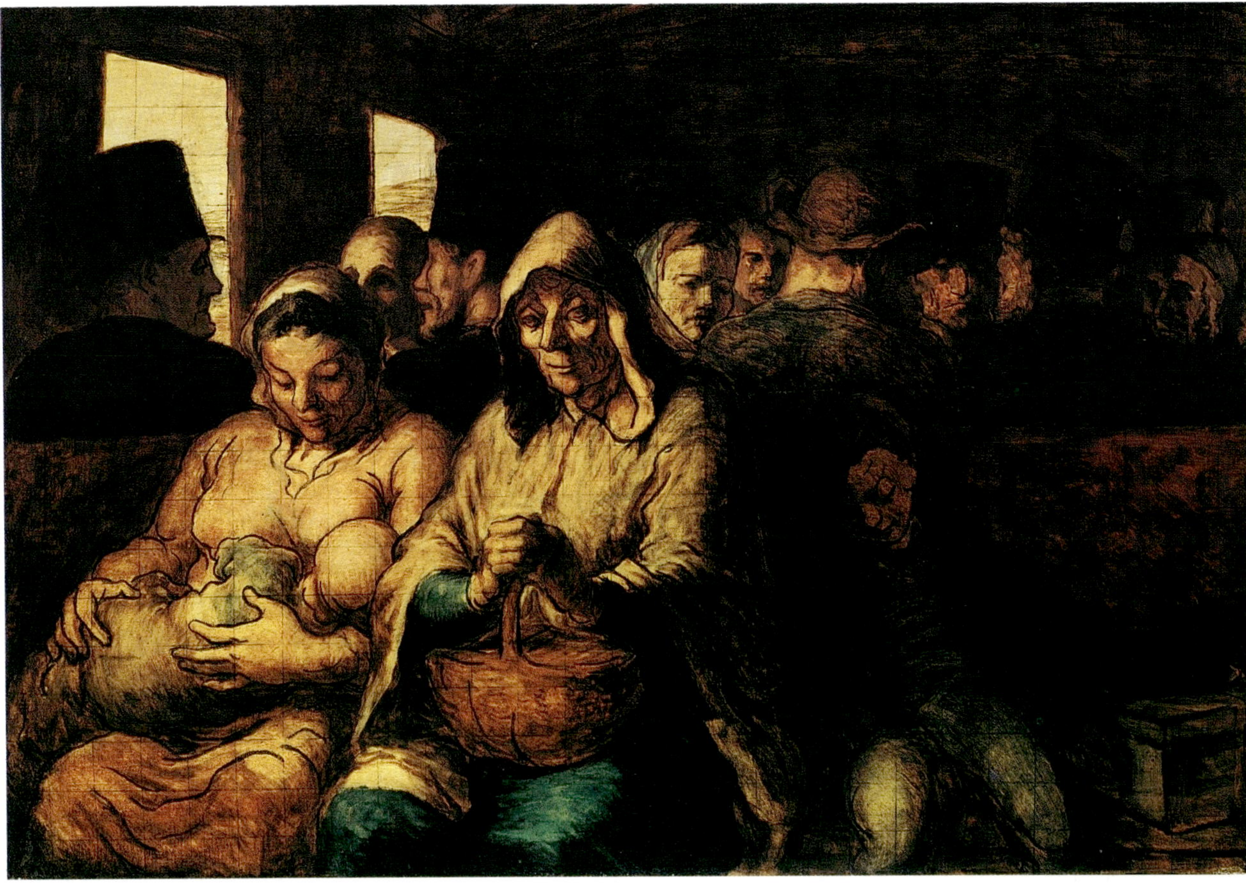

◆ HONORÉ DAUMIER
Third-Class Carriage
(1862-64, New York, Museum of Modern Art).
In this scene the eye of the artist concentrates on the resigned misery of the people, expressed through the extremely contorted, undulating lines.

◆ FISHERMAN ON THE BEACH
(1883, Otterlo, Rijksmuseum Kröller-Müller).
The fisherman, of extraordinary plastic synthesis, is caught during a moment of rest. The thick brush-stroke hides the face of the figure, almost as if trying to deprive it of all identity.

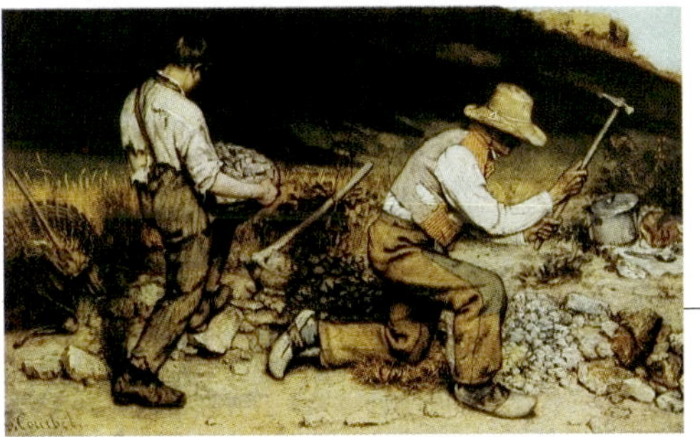

◆ GUSTAVE COURBET
Stone Breakers
(1849, formerly in Dresden, the work was destroyed during the Second World War).
The French artist's crude, polemical realism has always been controversial. Courbet, in fact, rejected the lyricism with which his contemporaries depicted manual workers in favor of the representation of hard work and exhaustion, as in the two figures portrayed here.

◆ THE POTATO EATERS
(1885, Amsterdam, Rijksmuseum Vincent Van Gogh).
Undoubtedly one of the artist's most famous works, *The Potato Eaters* (of which he produced three versions) is like a manifesto of his early output. The intense feeling for the hardship of the peasants is evident in the measured language and the absolute lack of contact between the figures, either verbal or eye contact. The dramatic intensity of the scene is also enhanced by the gesture with which the lean hands of the workers peel the potatoes.

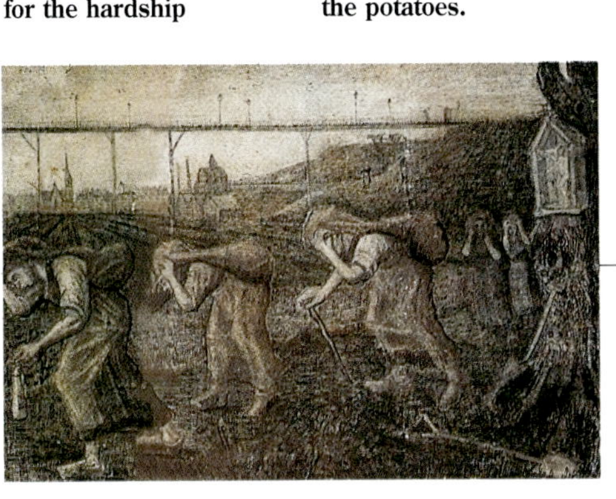

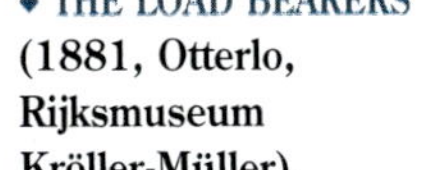

◆ THE LOAD BEARERS
(1881, Otterlo, Rijksmuseum Kröller-Müller).
The figures, unrecognizable due to their pose, move along with slow, visibly weary steps. The only comfort in a life without hope is the faith in the crucifix.

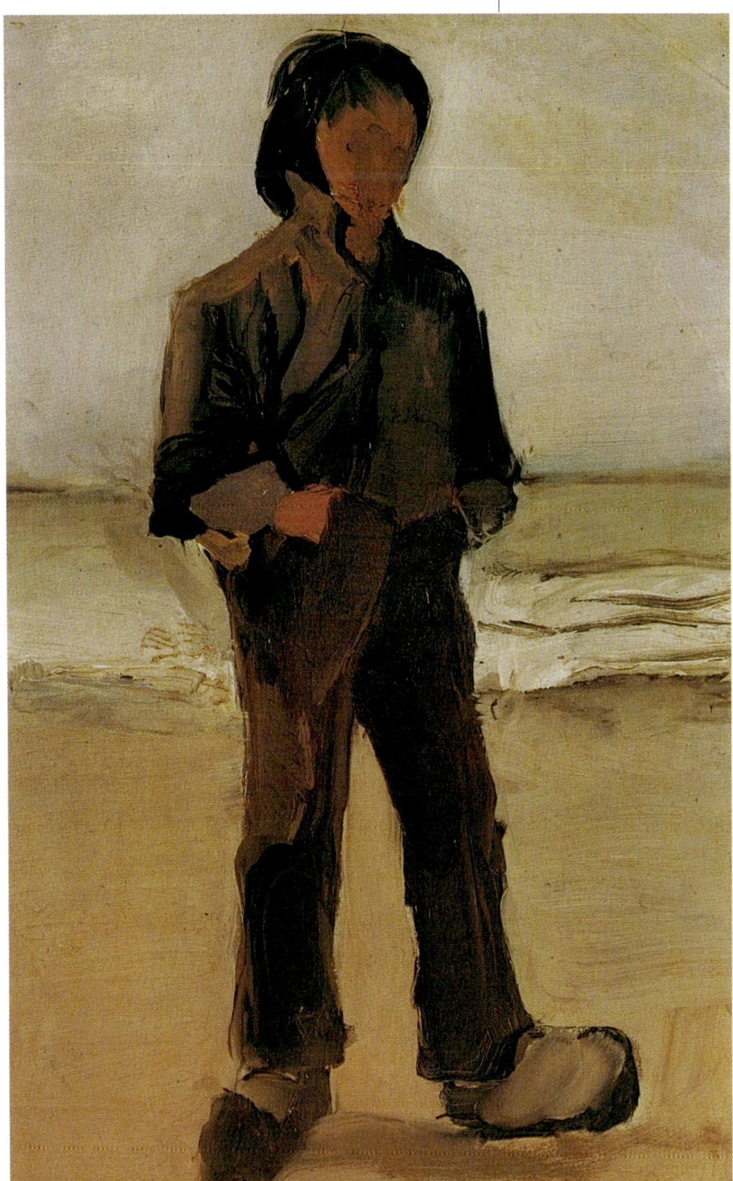

STILL LIFES

The key to Van Gogh's power lies in the extreme simplicity of his communicative means. His images spring from the flux of life, and in this sense his still lifes are typical. In the manner of metonym or metaphor, they represent reality through the depiction of a part or through personification, as when he evokes the memory of his absent friend Gauguin by means of his empty chair, or when he alludes to himself by including his hat in the painting.

● The elementary life of peasants is synthesized in the Christian symbols and the secular naturalism of *Still Life with*

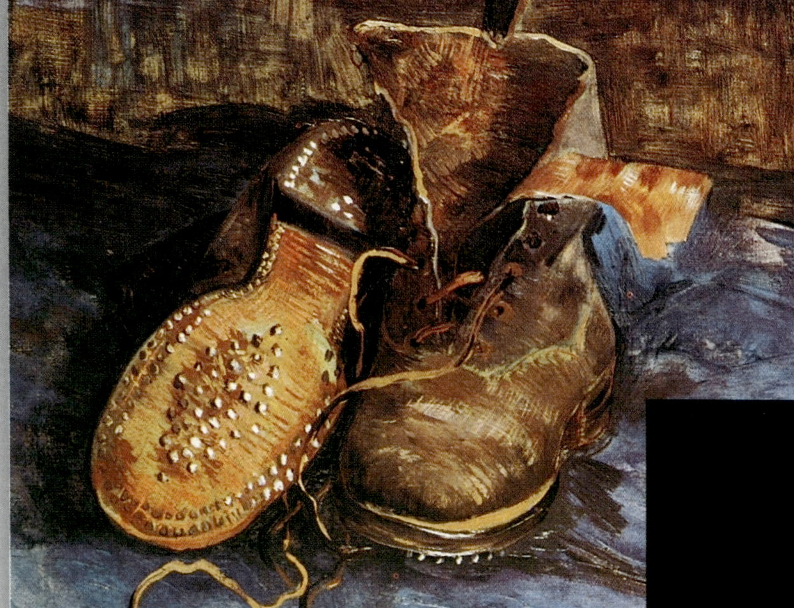

Bible, where the humility and the need for comfort are juxtaposed with Zola's *La Joie de vivre*. The dark side of this harsh life is underlined by the snuffed candle, an allusion to death. Elsewhere Van Gogh depicted the poor exclusively through their food: onions and potatoes.

● Van Gogh also applied his simple, everyday esthetics to shoes, a theme that derived from his interest in the poor classes, but that was also linked to the great tradition of European painting as exemplified by the clogs of the peasants portrayed by Millet. Van Gogh, however, replaced the descriptive analysis of his predecessor with poetic synthesis contained in a single element; the detail of the shoes, in fact, evokes the harsh life of the workers and the metaphorical wandering of their lives. As Heidegger pointed out, the deformed, muddy shoes sum up the exalted essence of truth, in the same way that Caravaggio had managed to capture the symbols of the tragic lives and the faith of the poor in the dirty feet of the pilgrims. The Dutch artist, too, was well aware that the first poor wanderer on earth was Jesus himself.

● In other works, large vases of flowers stand triumphant in the middle of the canvas and in the foreground. The simplicity of these compositions ensures their immediacy, while the bright, vibrant colors convey a sense of joy. In the details, however, Van Gogh returns to the *memento mori*; a broken flower, a twisted stalk, the sharp profile of a flower, or a sudden cold tone in the midst of the prevailing warm colors, yellow and red.

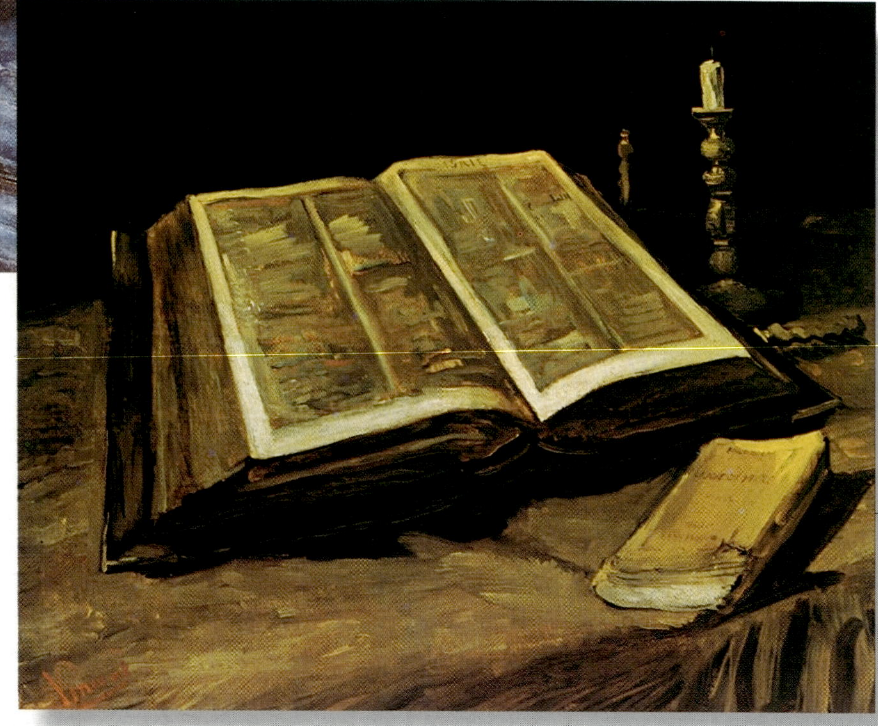

◆ VINCENT VAN GOGH AND EMILE BERNARD
The photo shows Van Gogh with his back turned as he talks to his friend Emile Bernard, the Synthetist painter and colleague of Gauguin.
The two artists are seen in Asnières in 1886, during Van Gogh's stay in Paris, when he frequently met up with other painters.

◆ VINCENT'S CHAIR WITH HIS PIPE
(1888, London, Tate Gallery).
The painter represents himself through his own world: the box of onions in the corner, which bears his signature, the floor of the modest room, and the plain chair with his pipe.

◆ A PAIR OF SHOES
(1887, Baltimore, Museum of Art).
Van Gogh bought the shoes at a second-hand market and wore them specially to get them dirty in order to enhance the symbolic power of the representation.

◆ STILL LIFE WITH BIBLE
(1885, Amsterdam, Rijksmuseum Vincent Van Gogh).
The image still possesses the gloomy style and strong chiaroscuro contrasts typical of his early work in Holland.
The objects convey poetically the values of a humble existence: faith, life and death.

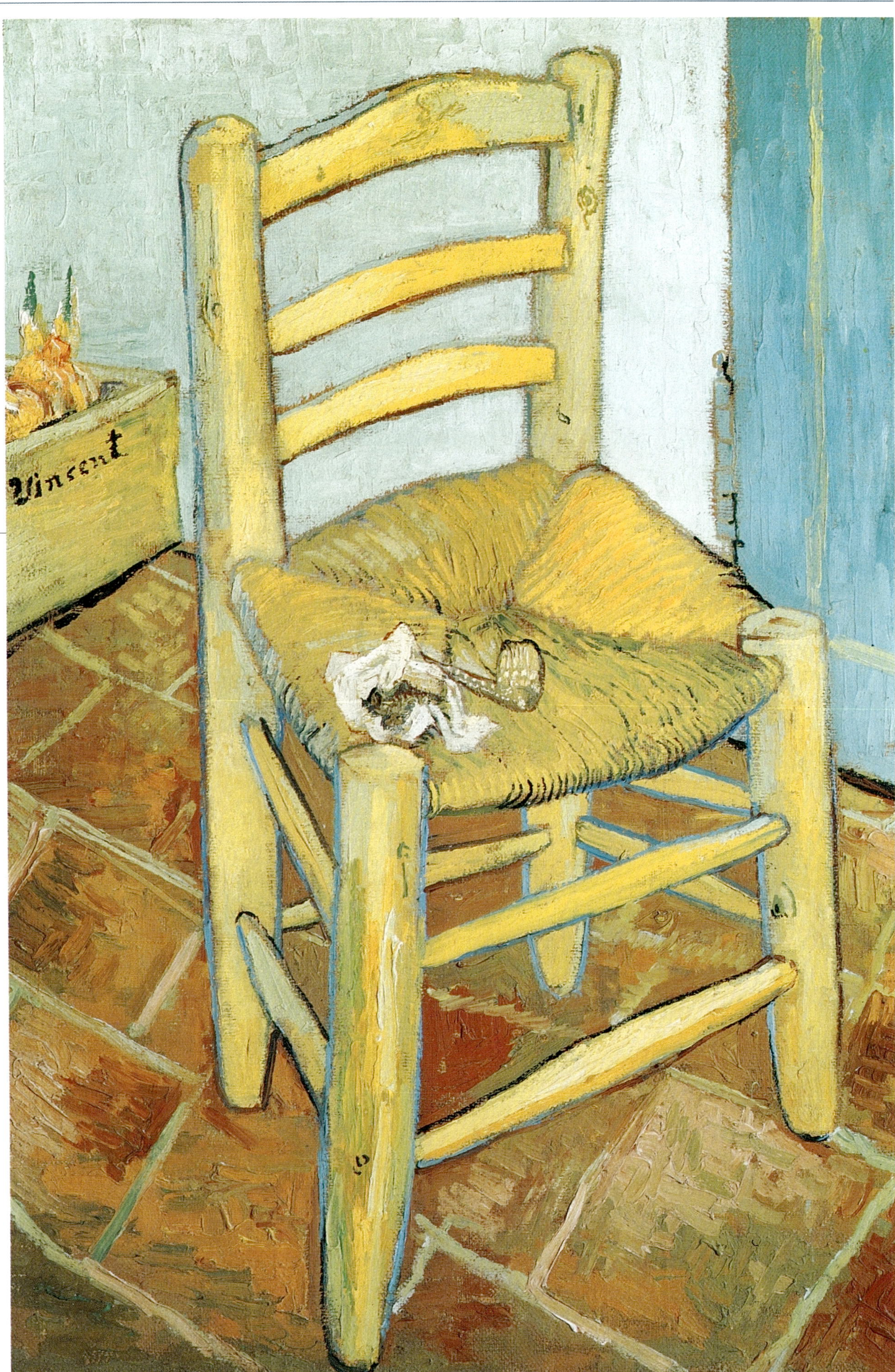

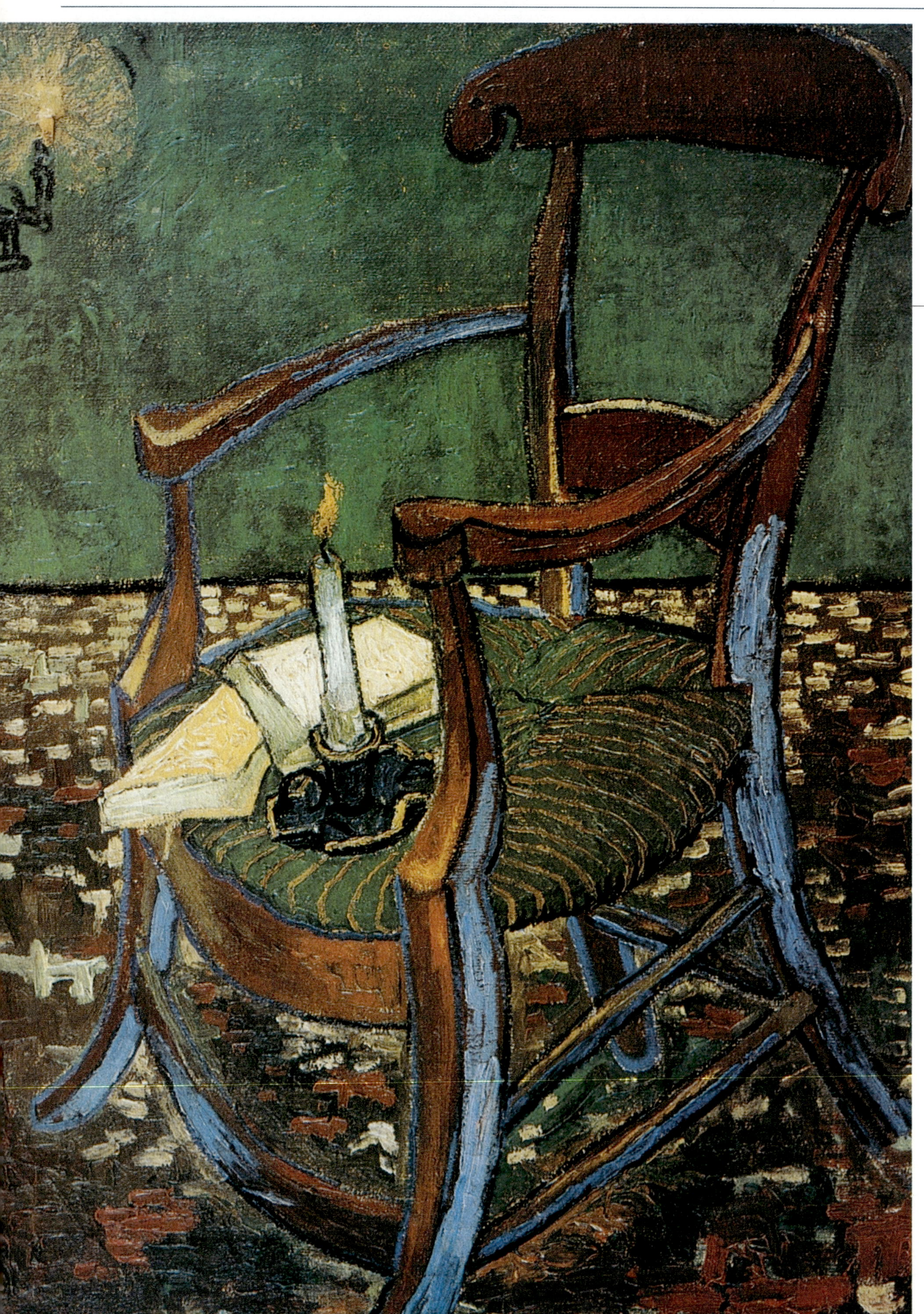

◆PAUL GAUGUIN'S ARMCHAIR (1888, Amsterdam, Rijksmuseum Vincent Van Gogh). Compared to its twin *Van Gogh's Chair*, this chair is explicitly refined. The simplicity of the first painting contrasts with this finer, more decorative image. The pipe and the onions are replaced with a candle and some books, an allusion to culture and intellectual liveliness. While the previous self-portrait is rendered through his customary objects, the element underlined here is his solitude in the absence of his friend.

◆ IRISES (1890, Amsterdam, Rijksmuseum Vincent Van Gogh). During this period Van Gogh produced a number of paintings of irises, mainly depicted in gardens, where their expressive power is more intense. Here the joyful theme is balanced by the bent flowers, a note of sadness in the overall blaze of jubilant color. Once again Van Gogh uses primary colors, exalted by their juxtaposition and also by the harmony with the green that they create together.

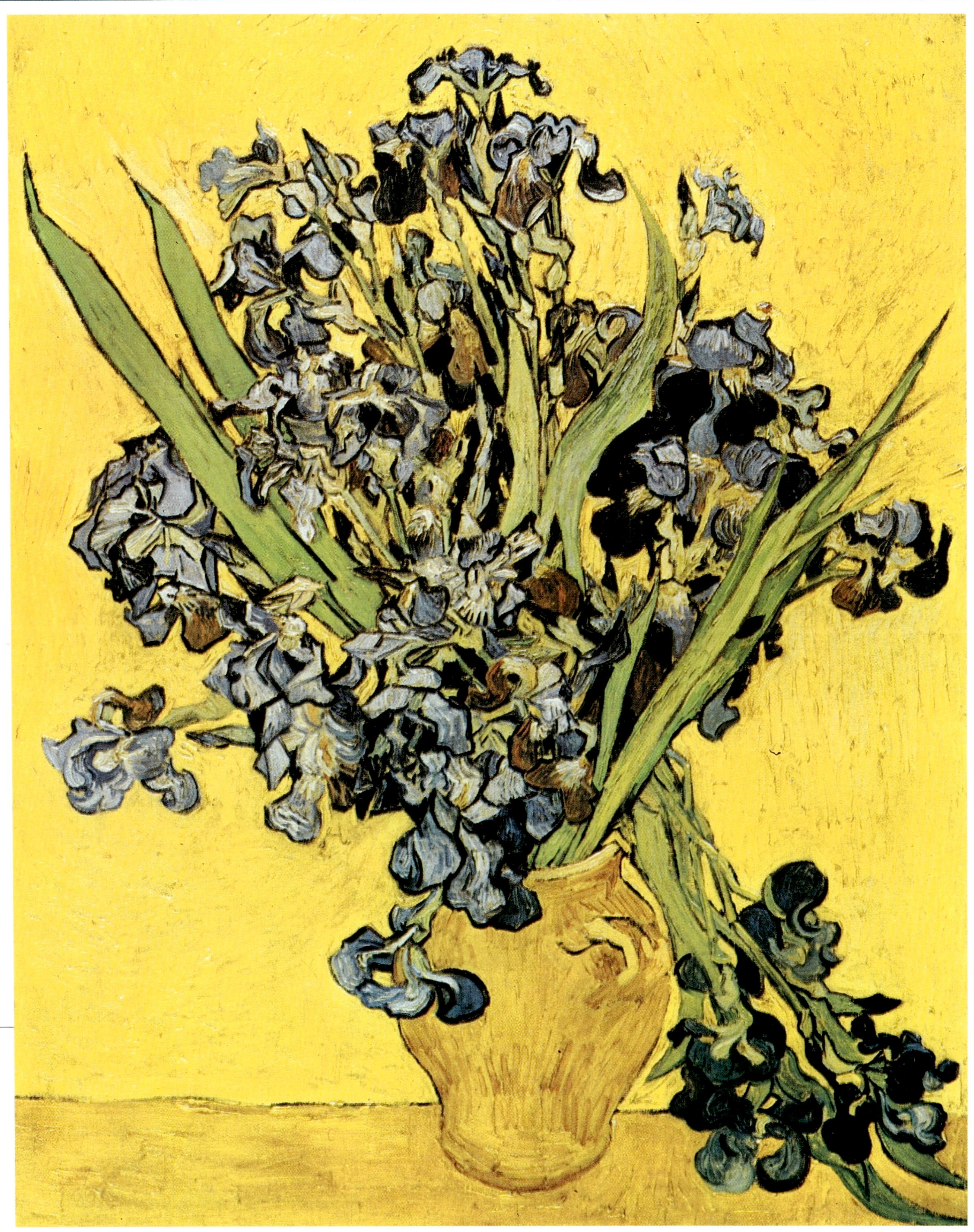

FROM IMPRESSIONISM TO NEO-IMPRESSIONISM

When Van Gogh arrived in Paris in 1886, the last exhibition of Impressionism was opening, also including the work of the new generation of neo-Impressionists. The two movements marked a definitive break with academic rules and paved the way to a form of art animated by a new interest in modern reality and by greater creative spontaneity.

● Painters were leaving their ateliers in order to come into direct, immediate contact with nature *en plein air*, without any academic filter, breaking the rules consecrated by tradition. Through the scientific discoveries of Blanc and Charles Henry, the Impressionists made light the dominant feature of their canvases, abolished local color and reconstructed the fleeting hues that result from the interaction of intense luminosity, adjacent colors and weather conditions.

● The shortened brush-stroke of the Impressionists, with the lively rhythm of brief, curved touches, was the defining feature of the painting of Seurat. The French master reduced the small lines of color to an expanse of dots. Through a strict scientific grid based on the juxtaposition of complementary colors, he offered a less intuitive interpretation of chromatic division and of the *ductus*.

● Van Gogh thus discovered the potentialities inherent in color and learnt to make the surface of the painting vibrate by spreading a layer of mosaic-like colors. From his Parisian colleagues, he sometimes also took certain themes drawn from contemporary life, like the women sitting in cafes or the bridges over rivers, though he always reworked them in an original way, creating unexpected variations in technique and symbolism.

● In 1887 the Dutch master exhibited with Bernard, Gauguin and Toulouse-Lautrec in what was defined as the group of the "Petit Boulevard Painters", while in 1889 he was present with ten paintings at the *Salon des Indépendants*. For Van Gogh, however, the contact with the Parisian avant-garde of the eighties was not a point of arrival, but a starting point for a new, entirely personal development.

◆ HENRI TOULOUSE-LAUTREC *Vincent Van Gogh* **(1887, Amsterdam, Rijksmuseum Vincent Van Gogh). In Paris, Lautrec and Van Gogh took part together in the cafe society.**

THE PARTNERSHIP WITH GAUGUIN

When Gauguin arrived in Arles on 31 October 1888, for Van Gogh it was the fulfillment of a dream. The longed-for community of artists seemed to have been realized, his solitude was over, and his painting had found a maestro. The artists spent two intense months together, painting the same subjects (like Madame Ginoux). Gauguin was working towards synthetic forms and flat colors of a symbolist nature; Van Gogh was trying to depict concrete reality with bright tones and thick brush-strokes. Gauguin would later recall: "When I arrived in Arles Vincent was floundering in neo-Impressionism. I tried to help him, which was easy since I found a rich and fertile terrain." Gradually, however, the atmosphere filled with an "excessive electricity" and relations became tense until things came to a head on 23 December, when Vincent attacked his friend in a fit of ire. For Van Gogh the end of the partnership coincided with the beginning of a terrifying period of solitude, worsened by incomprehension.

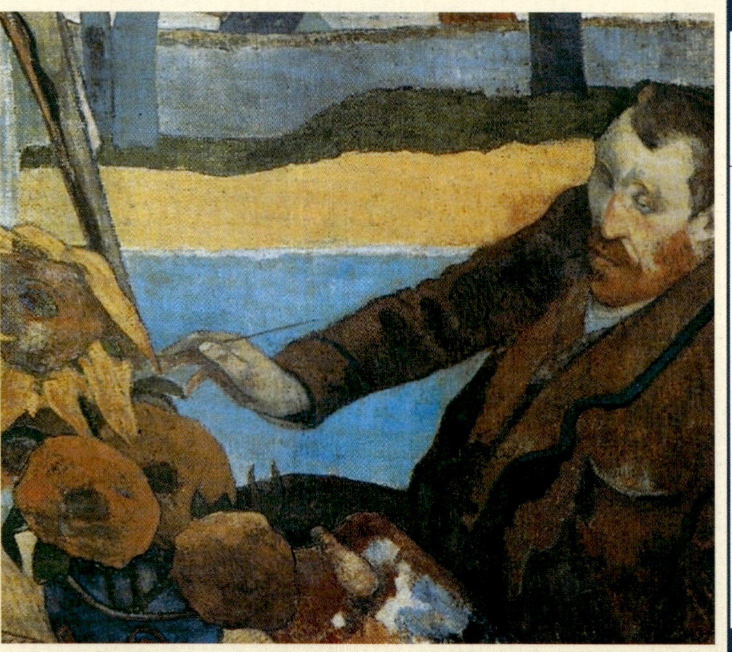

◆ PAUL GAUGUIN *Van Gogh Painting Sunflowers* **(1888, Amsterdam, Rijksmuseum Vincent Van Gogh). During this period Gauguin was developing a synthetic, flat style, enhanced here by the angle of the composition.**

◆ INTERIOR OF A RESTAURANT **(1887, Otterlo, Rijksmuseum Kröller-Müller). In the subject, the Divisionist style and the vibrant colors, the work shows the evident influence of neo-Impressionism.**

THE INFLUENCE OF JAPANESE ART

Japanese culture began to invade Europe in 1853, when the gates to the country were opened. The exoticism and singularity of Japanese art led it to triumph in Europe and made it fashionable in France after the Universal Expositions of 1876, 1878 and 1889. Based around the shop run by Sigfried Bing (who Van Gogh knew), there was a flourishing trade in Japanese handicraft, clothes and prints. In art circles, the Japanese influence involved the adoption of an à plat style and of perspectives based on diagonal lines. This brought about the abandonment of traditional perspective and of the hierarchy of values linked to it, allowing the recovery of decorative elements as well as of a brighter palette. In assimilating the suggestions of Japanese art, Van Gogh was joined by Monet, Degas, Whistler and Toulouse-Lautrec, who were all reflecting on the new developments. Van Gogh's interest, however, went beyond stylistic motivations: he was, in fact, seeking to emulate the ideal of community in Japanese culture.

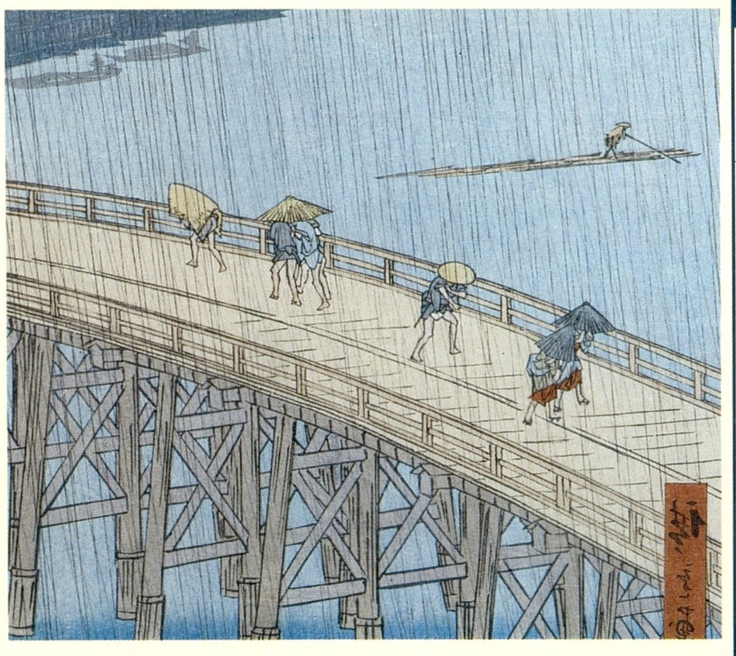

◆ HIROSHIGE
Ohashi Bridge in the Rain
(1857, Paris, Musée Guimet).
The bridge, the metaphor of passage as existential growth, shows the Japanese predilection for the diagonal and creates a powerful sense of unity.

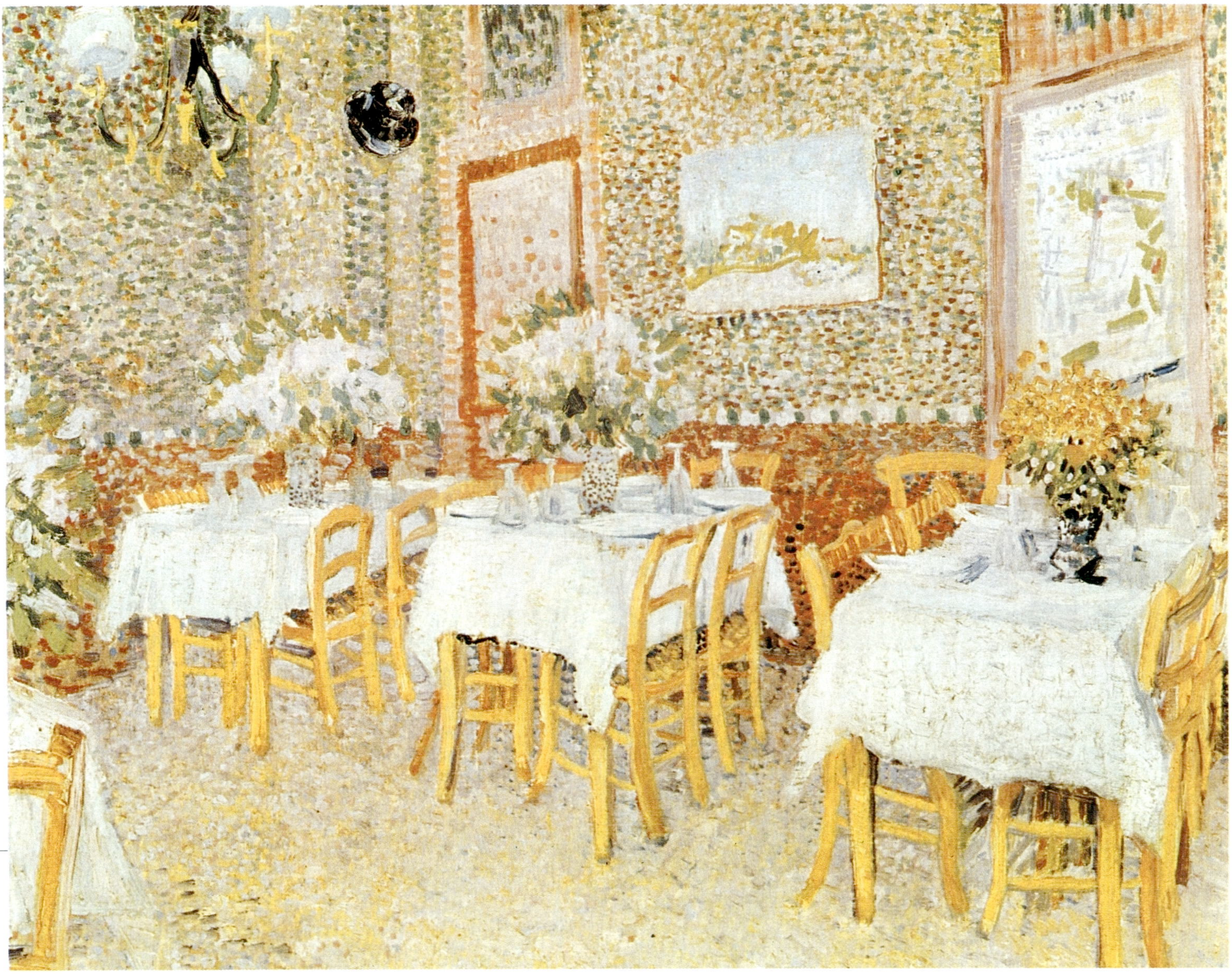

♦ THE LANGLOIS BRIDGE AT ARLES (1888, Cologne, Wallraf-Richartz Museum). The theme of the bridge is drawn from Japanese art. The two-dimensionality of the lines is exploited to construct the image. The light, spring colors are also taken from Oriental prints. Van Gogh produced four oil paintings of the same subject, as well as a number of watercolor studies.

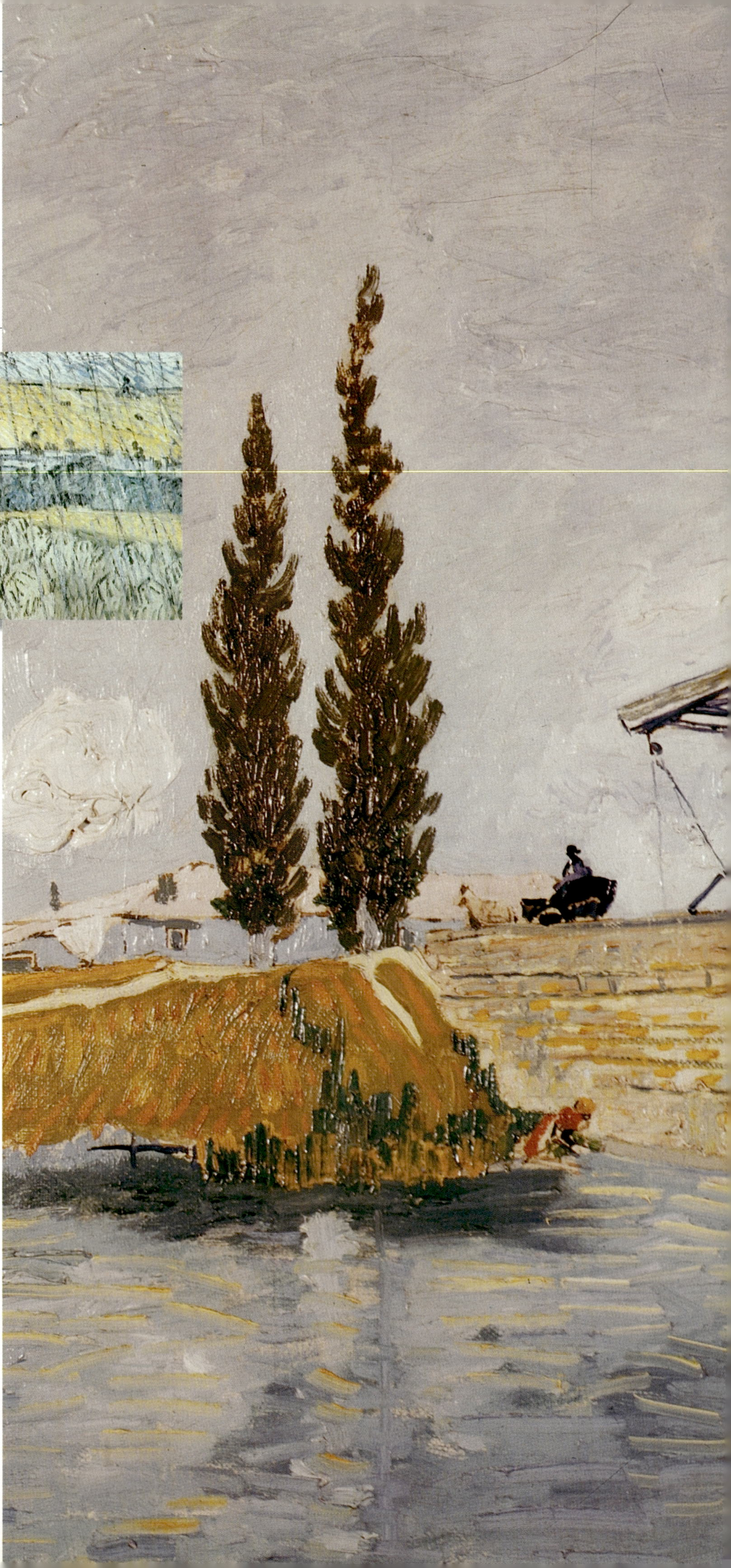

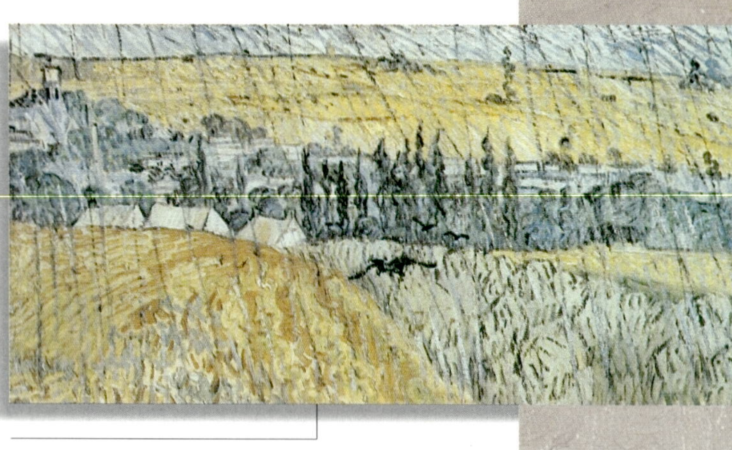

♦ LANDSCAPE AT AUVERS IN THE RAIN (1890, Cardiff, National Museum of Wales). In this canvas, which uses the rain to simulate the graininess of a wooden table, Van Gogh experiments in a very personal way with elements drawn from Japanese culture. The horizontal character of the painting and the absence of human figures create a profound sense of solitude.

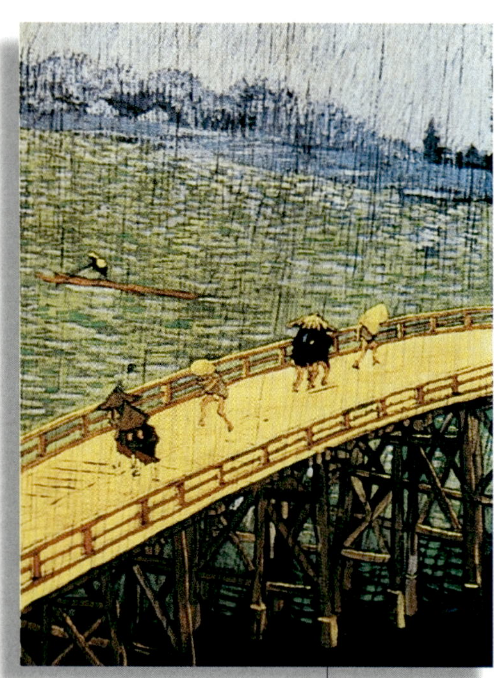

♦ JAPONAISERIE: BRIDGE IN THE RAIN (AFTER HIROSHIGE) (1887, Amsterdam, Rijksmuseum Vincent Van Gogh). The painting reproduces Hiroshige's woodcut of 1857, of which Van Gogh owned a copy. He was fascinated by the sharp, apparently simple lines.

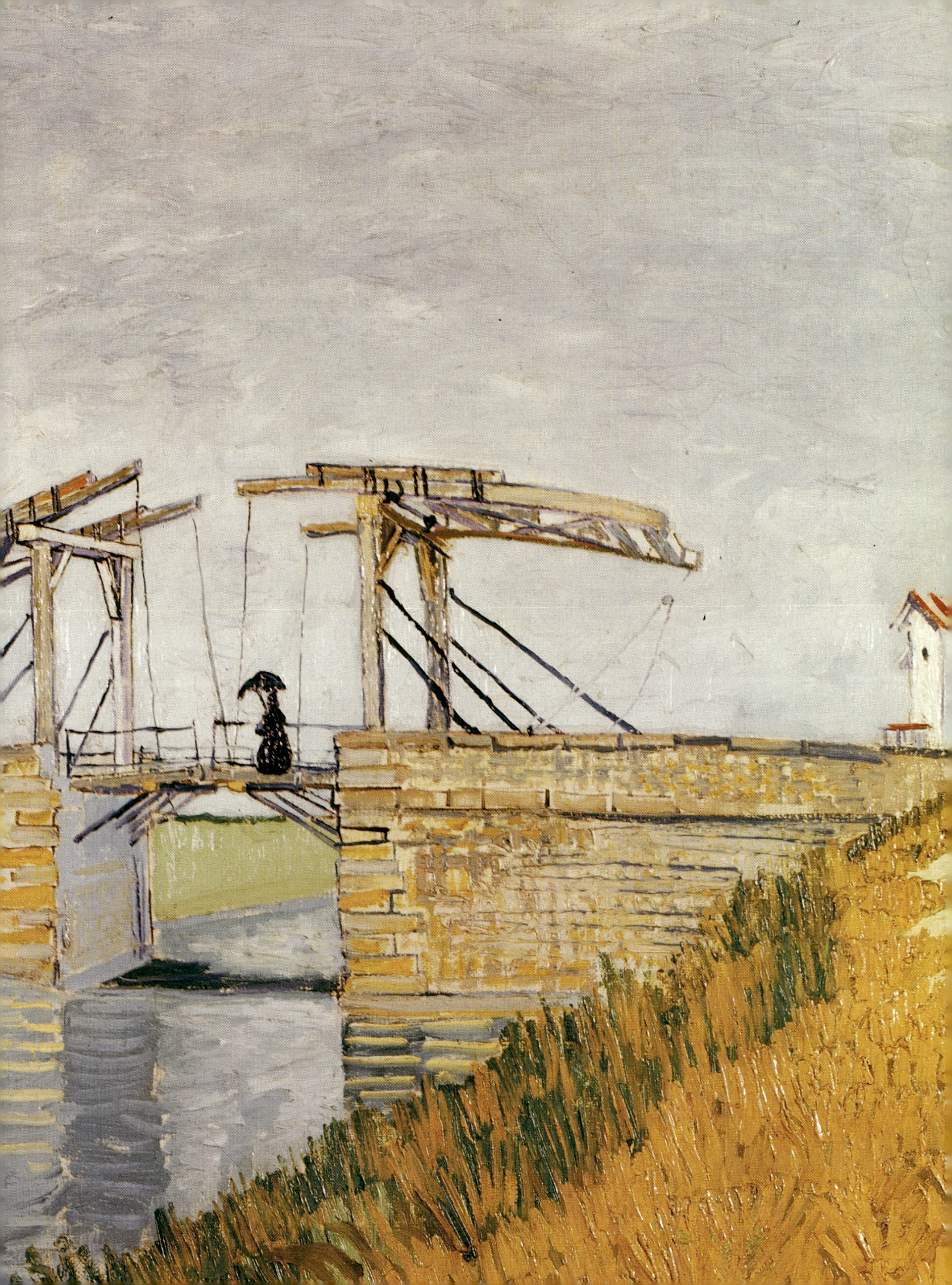

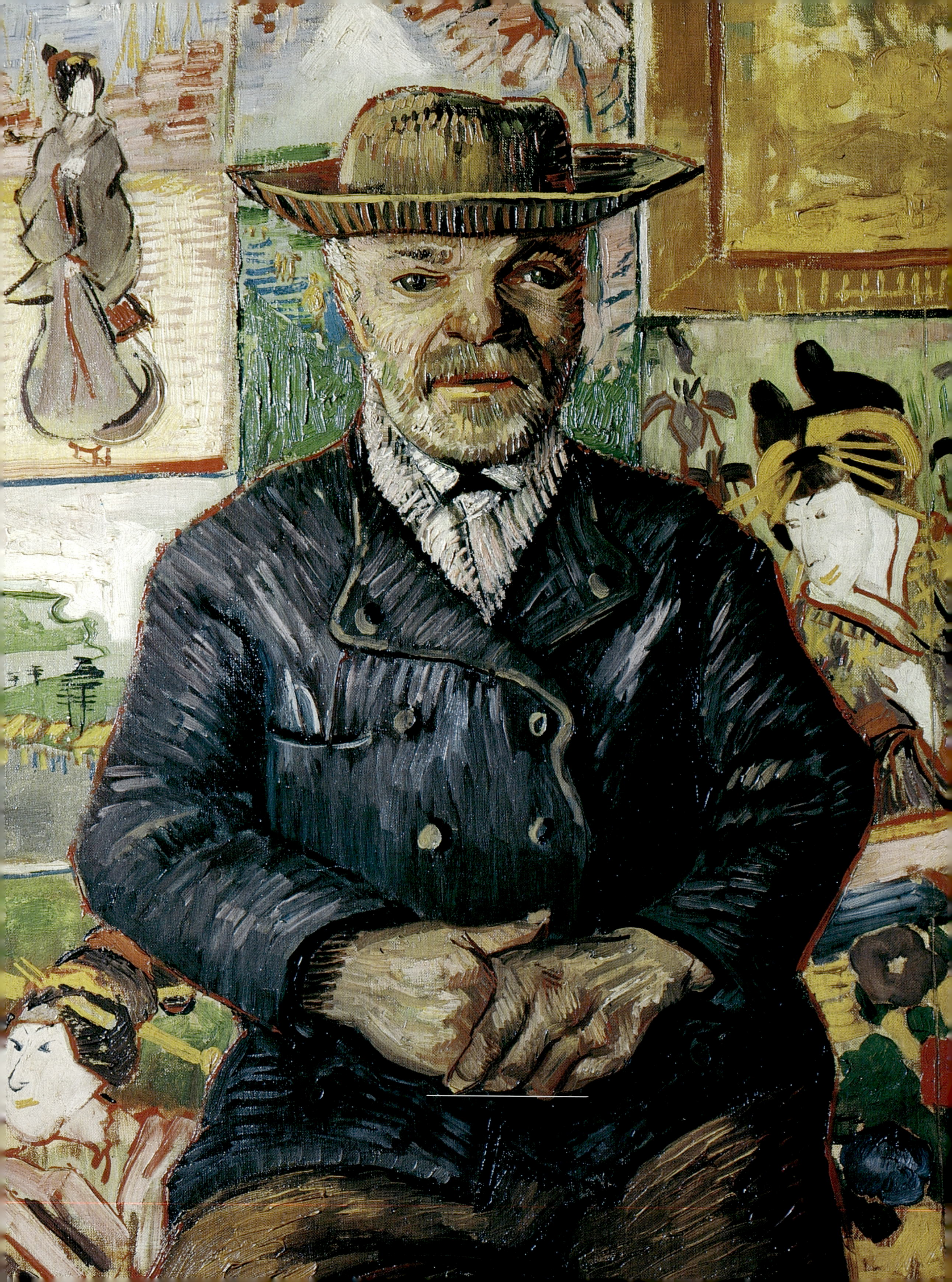

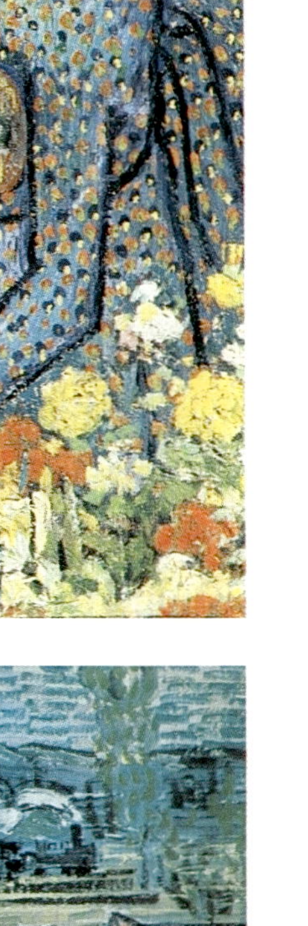

◆ TWO WOMEN (MEMORY OF THE GARDEN AT ETTEN) (1888, St. Petersburg, Hermitage). The work was painted in Arles, during Gauguin's stay. In *Garden in Arles*, Gauguin translates the density of Van Gogh's subject with an individual, highly synthetic style.

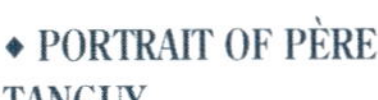

◆ PORTRAIT OF PÈRE TANGUY (1887, Athens, Stavros S. Niarchos Collection). This portrait once again demonstrates the artist's passion for Oriental culture, though we can also see traces of Manet's portrait of Zola: there, too, the background is made up of Japanese prints.

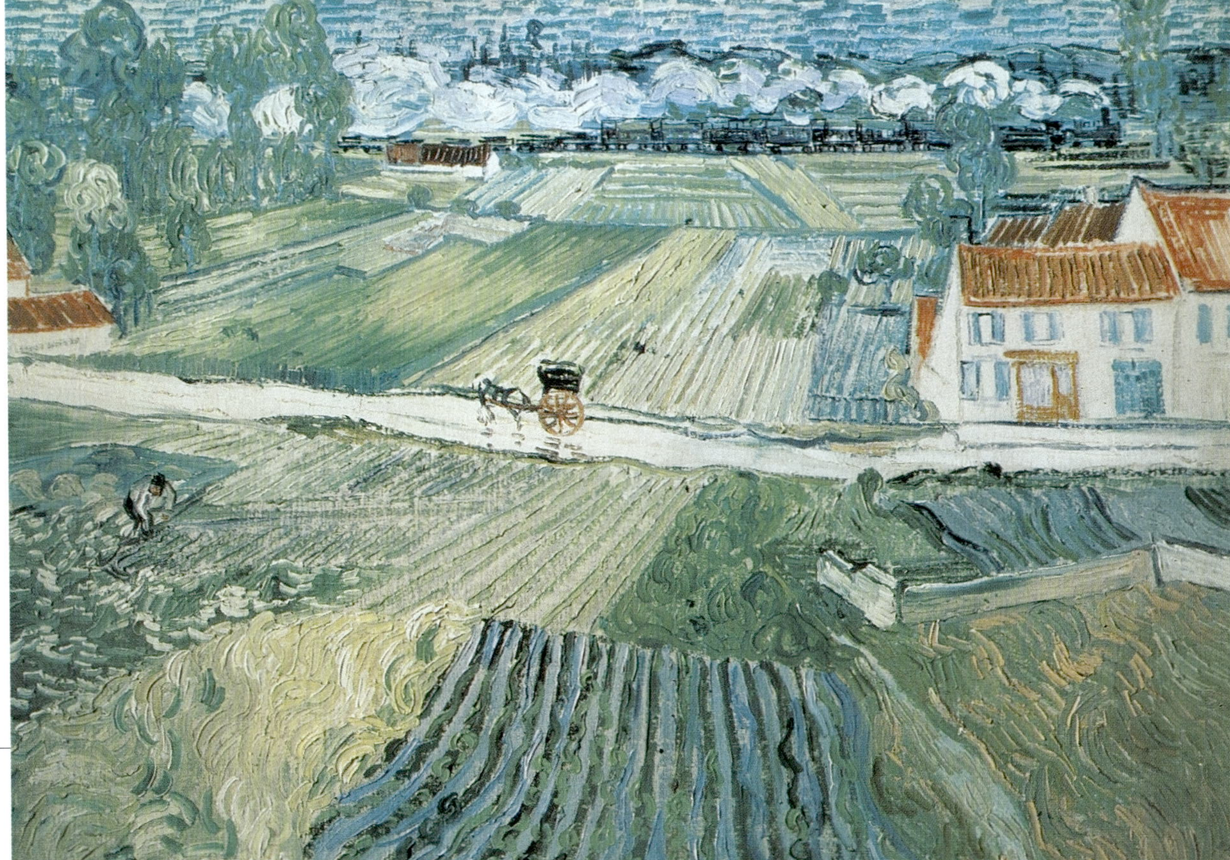

◆ LANDSCAPE WITH CARRIAGE AND TRAIN IN THE BACKGROUND (1890, Moscow, Pushkin Museum). This landscape, with the train on the horizon, is reminiscent of the works of Monet. The human figures disappear in the immensity of nature.

THE IMAGE OF PEASANT SPIRITUALITY

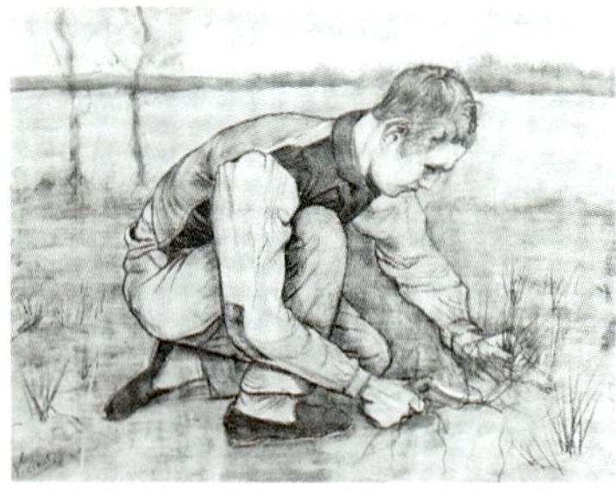

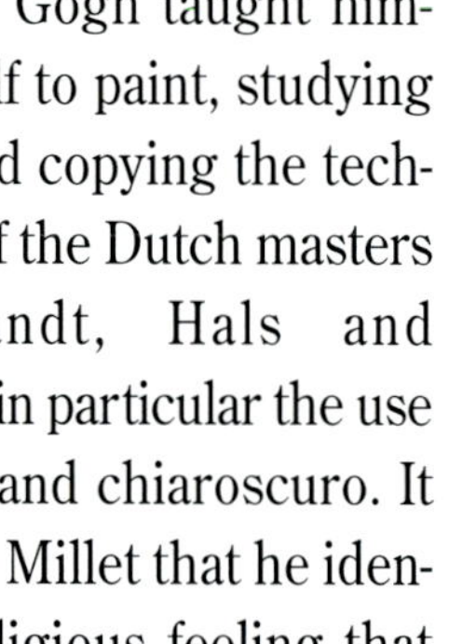

Van Gogh taught himself to paint, studying and copying the techniques of the Dutch masters Rembrandt, Hals and Rubens, in particular the use of color and chiaroscuro. It was, however, with the work of François Millet that he identified most closely: attracted by the religious feeling that pervades the French master's canvases, he reproduced the indissoluble, brutal link between man and nature in a endless series of variations on the theme.

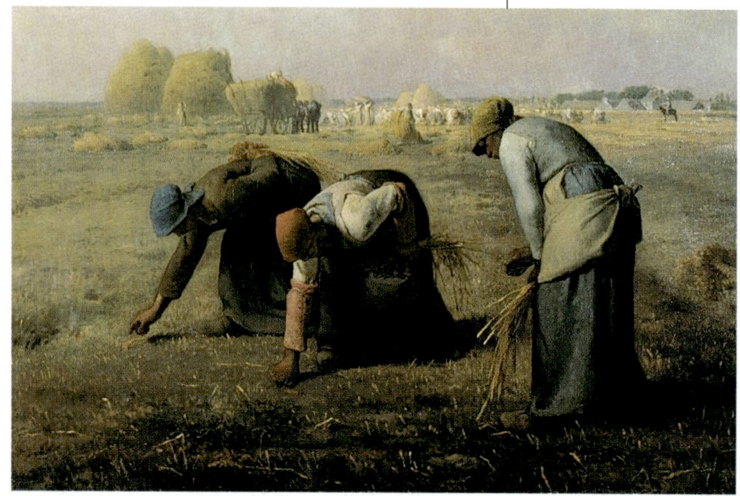

♦ JEAN-FRANÇOIS MILLET
The Gleaners
(1857, Paris, Louvre). In the repetition of the movement there is a sort of sacred rite that annuls any apparent exhaustion.

● Van Gogh felt at home with the values of rural life rather than city life, and in the iconography of Millet he found the themes of toil and the immutability of life which he had been seeking. He began with faithful copies of Millet's sowers and peasants, exaggerating their outlines: the curved though gentle forms of Millet are turned into more undulating, tormented profiles. His lines seem to blend the tension learned from Daumier's caricatures with Millet's lyrical style.

● Van Gogh collected prints of Millet's work, finding in them a stimulus for his art and also the serenity of a familiar world. As his health deteriorated in Saint-Rémy, he was often forced to give up his walks in the fields, during which he would look for subjects to paint. And at those times his collection, regularly updated with new prints of Japanese artists and of Millet sent to him by his brother Theo, became the only alternative to self-portraits, and also an indispensable opportunity to escape from his prison and his suffering.

♦ PEASANT WITH SICKLE
(1881, Otterlo, Rijksmuseum Kröller-Müller). Van Gogh's sharp outlines add emphasis and drama to the gentler forms of Millet's peasants.

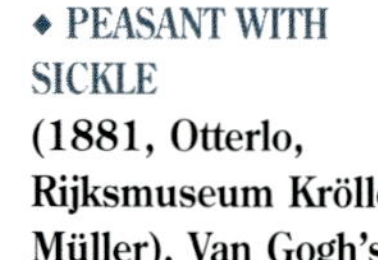

♦ JEAN-FRANÇOIS MILLET
Siesta
(1865-68, Philadelphia, Museum of Art, below) Here Millet's elegance gives way to an unusually photographic style.

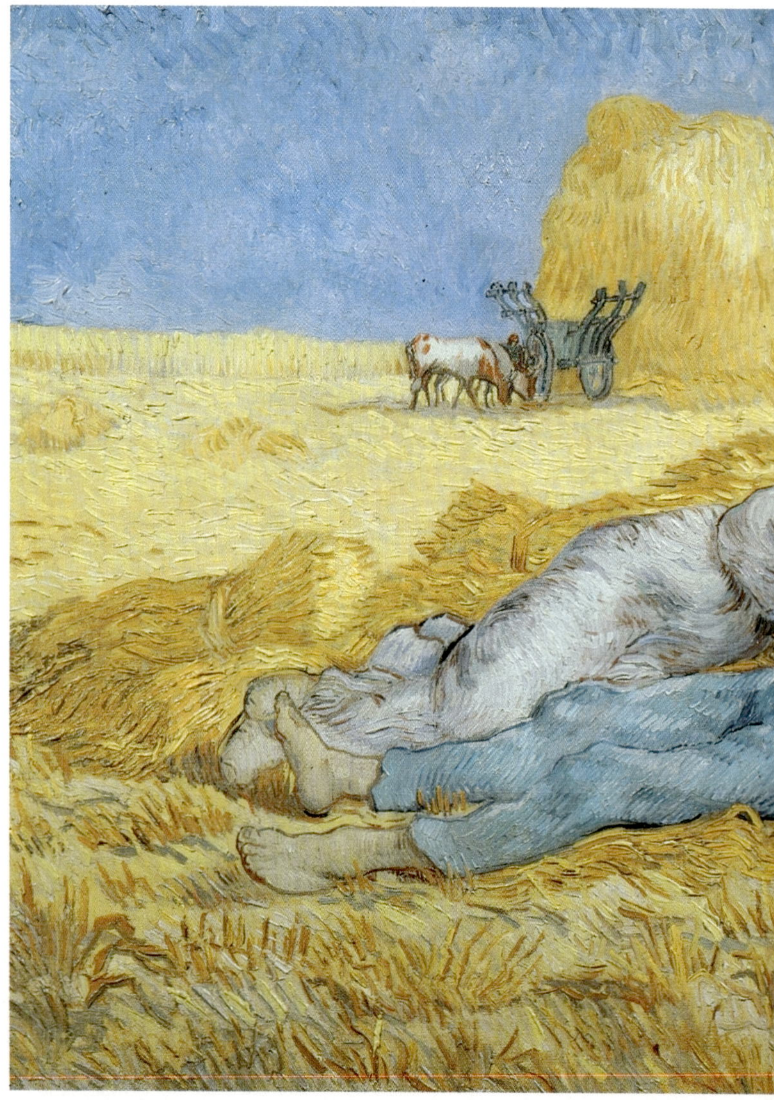

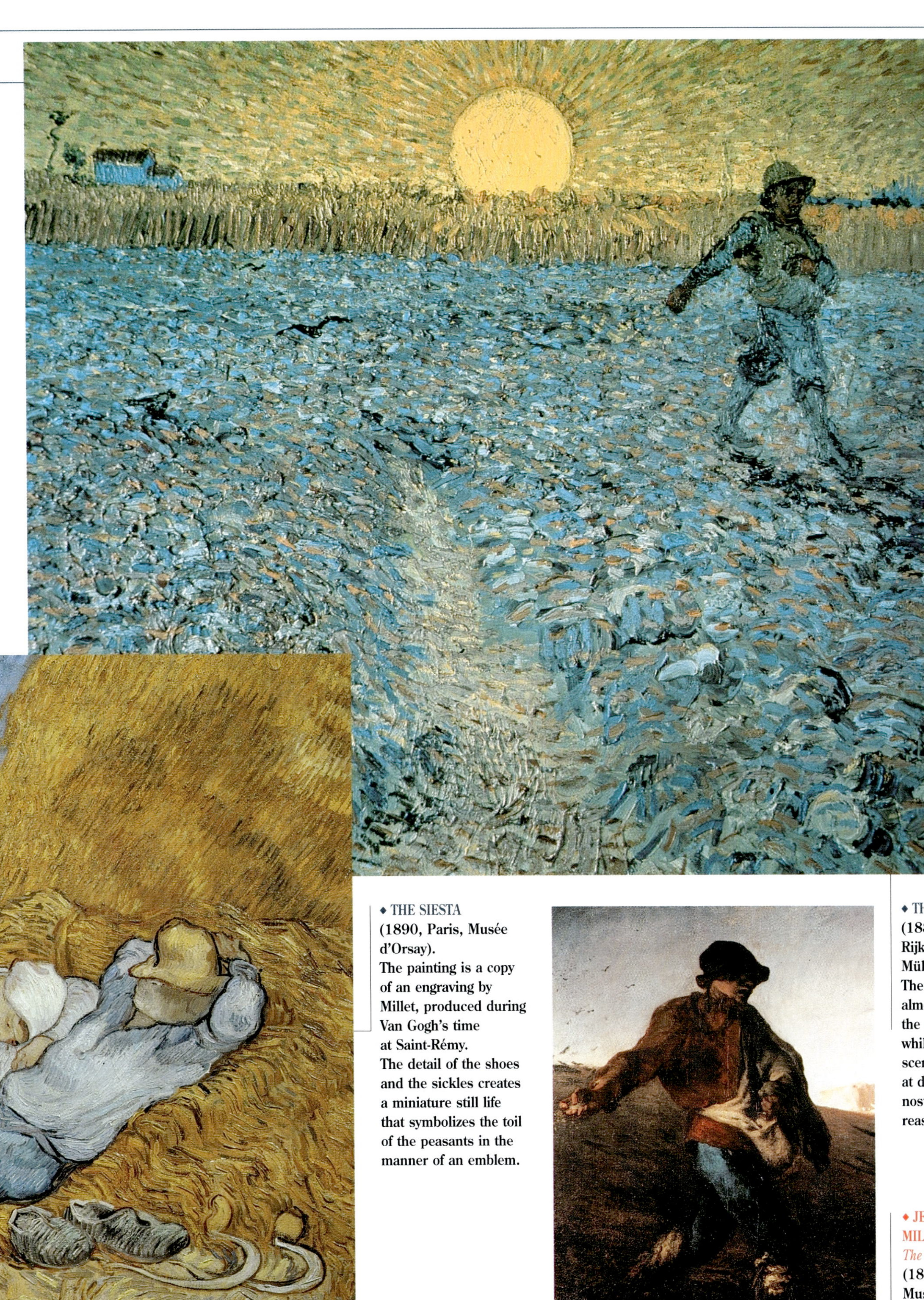

◆ THE SIESTA
(1890, Paris, Musée d'Orsay).
The painting is a copy of an engraving by Millet, produced during Van Gogh's time at Saint-Rémy.
The detail of the shoes and the sickles creates a miniature still life that symbolizes the toil of the peasants in the manner of an emblem.

◆ THE SOWER
(1888, Otterlo, Rijksmuseum Kröller-Müller).
The sower is copied almost faithfully from the model by Millet, while the background scene of the open field at dusk represents the nostalgic search for a reassuring nature.

◆ JEAN-FRANÇOIS MILLET
The Sower
(1850, Boston, Museum of Fine Arts).
In Millet's model, Van Gogh felt a spontaneous solidarity with the poors and their work.

THE TRIUMPH OF POSITIVISM AND SCIENCE

In the second half of the nineteenth century, science opened new horizons in terms of man's dominion over nature. From the use of natural fuels to the battle against disease, the development of science was translated into material progress for the benefit of society as a whole. Thus the well-being that came as a result seemed to be directly linked to scientific progress, attracting general interest. Positivism, with its appeal to knowledge based above all on the careful observation of empirical data, and with its faith in the methods and the developments of science, was not only a school of philosophy but also a general way of thinking. In this sense Positivism spread throughout Europe as a revolt against the old theological and metaphysical systems of thought, and against everything that had no evident social utility.

● This climate was characterized by the evolutionist theories of Charles Darwin, the great advances made by Louis Pasteur and Robert Koch in the field of medicine, the studies of radioactivity carried out by Marie and Pierre Curie, and the discoveries of Alexander Graham Bell and Guglielmo Marconi in the field of communications.

● There is also a close link between the direction taken by philosophical and scientific thought and the realism characteristic of the literature of the second half of the nineteenth century: we need only think, for example, of Charles Dickens or the naturalistic novels of Gustave Flaubert and Emile Zola, who Van Gogh loved. As a young man, before he turned to painting, Van Gogh had worked as a lay preacher among the Belgian miners. He had felt the powerful appeal of the work of Millet, especially its social content, so much so that he decided to become a painter himself.

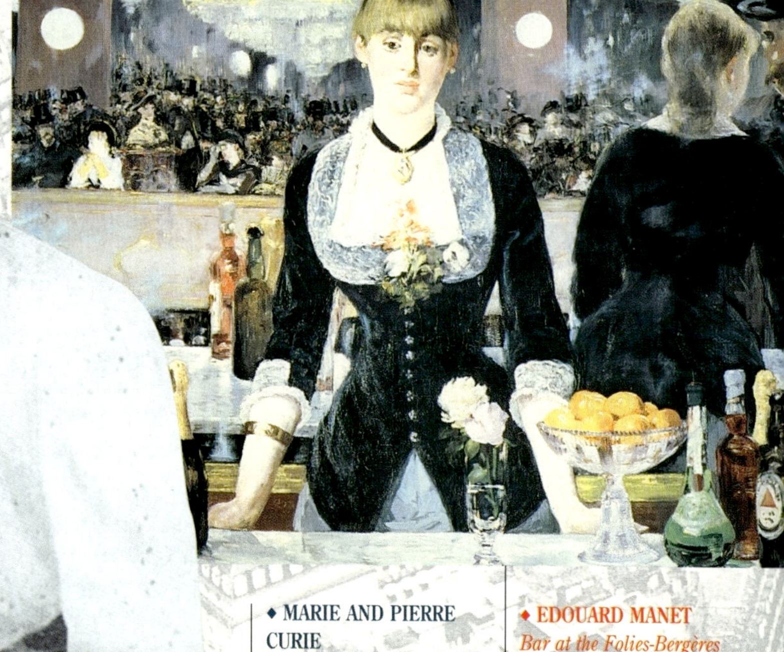

♦ MARIE AND PIERRE CURIE
The Curies were responsible for important studies on magnetism and radioactivity, leading to the invention of radium. In 1903 they were both awarded the Nobel Prize. Marie also obtained the award for her chemical research in 1911.

♦ EDOUARD MANET
Bar at the Folies-Bergères
(1881-82, London, Courtauld Institute of Art). Manet's name is linked with the entrance of modern life onto the scene of art. Few other artists have managed so well to render everyday subjects heroic and attractive.

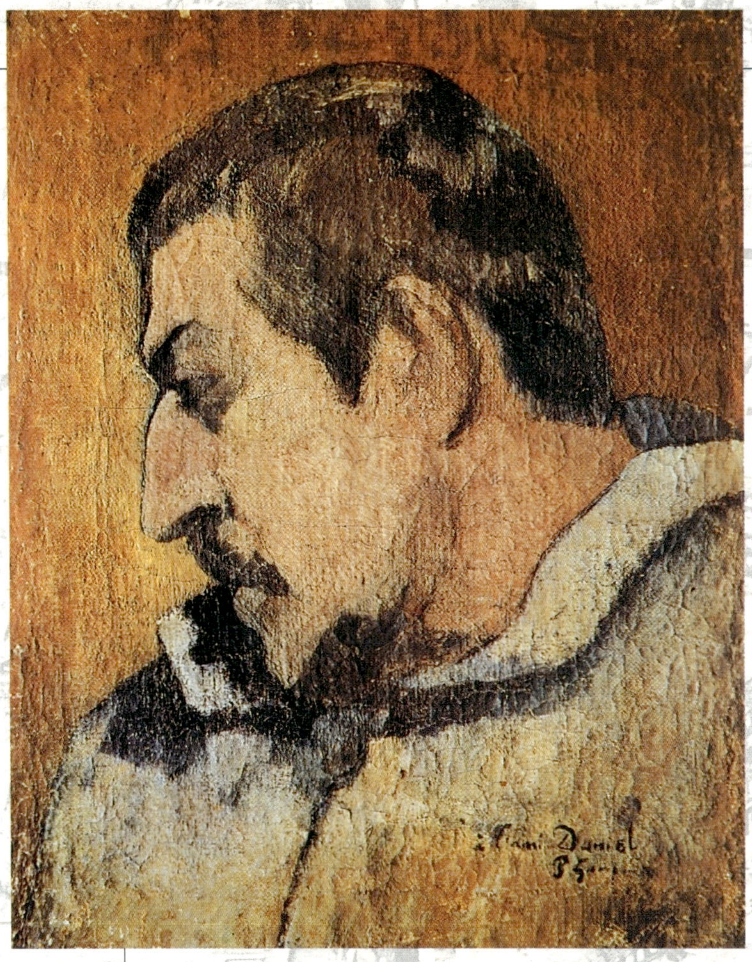

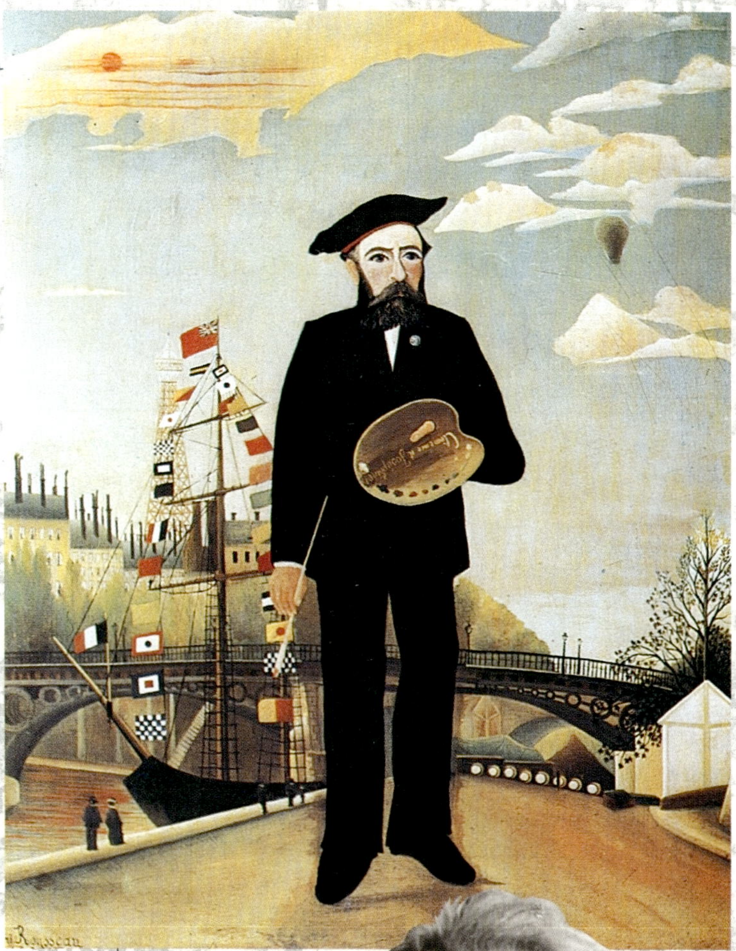

◆ PAUL GAUGUIN
Self-Portrait
(1896, Béziers, Collection M.me L. Huc de Monfreid).
Gauguin, once the great friend of Van Gogh, introduced a new development in modern art with the move towards decorative, highly synthetic effects that were a prelude to abstract art.
His flight to Polynesia was indicative of his rejection of Western civilization.

● Naturalistic subjects began to prevail in the field of art, too, firstly with the painting of Courbet and Millet and then with the Impressionists. However, the link with Positivism was even stronger, for scientific discoveries influenced the means of expression. Photography, a process which was becoming more practical with the first dagueurreotypes, was a clear influence on the visual and perceptive conception of Impressionism.

● The first exhibition of the Impressionists took place at the studio of the photographer Nadar in 1874, the year that marked the first industrial production of bromide plates for photography. On the other hand, the studies of color by M. Chevreul, who established important laws on the interaction of complementary colors, those of H. von Helmholtz, who focussed on the physiological mechanisms of the visual process, and finally the theories of C. Maxwell, who expounded the principle of additive synthesis, were decisive influences both for the neo-Impressionists and the Divisionists.

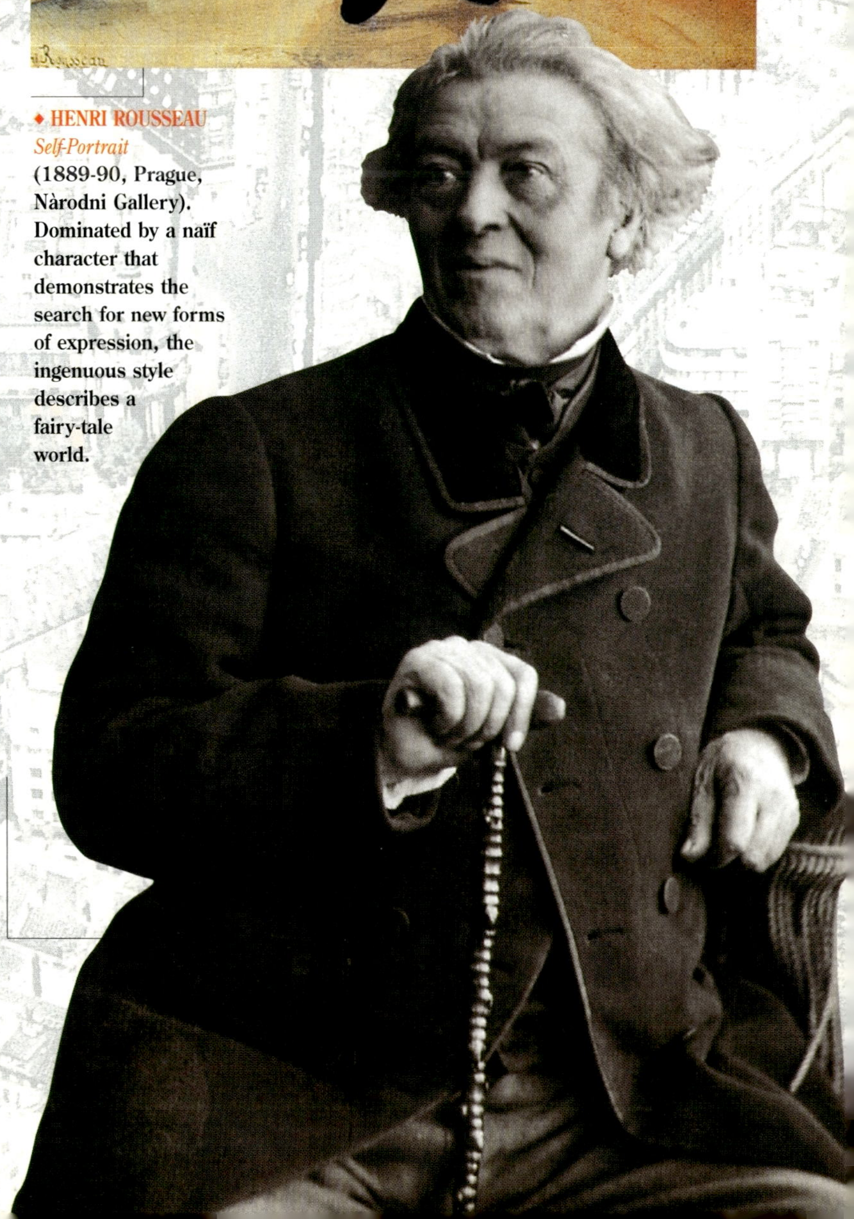

◆ HENRI ROUSSEAU
Self-Portrait
(1889-90, Prague, Nàrodni Gallery).
Dominated by a naïf character that demonstrates the search for new forms of expression, the ingenuous style describes a fairy-tale world.

◆ CAMILLE COROT
For the artists of the late nineteenth century, the work of Corot (1796-1875) constituted a fundamental point of reference due to his new interpretations of landscape and his studies on effects of light.

ON THE ROAD TO EXPRESSIONISM

The painful union of art and life in the work of Van Gogh, the rapture with which he traced the brush-stroke and his break with traditional forms, were destined to leave an indelible mark on twentieth-century painting, in particular on the first avant-garde movements. Thanks partly to the many retrospective exhibitions held around Europe, like the one in Berlin in 1910, his work obtained tardy, though widespread recognition.

● His emotional interpretation of reality, the violence of the colors that create and corrode the forms, and finally the exemplary and dramatic story of a man misunderstood by society, all played a role in the development of the Expressionist current in Germany. More than their colleagues in the *Blaue Reiter* group, with the exception of Jawlensky, it was the exponents of *Die Brücke* movement who showed themselves to be most susceptible to the influence of the Dutch master. In 1905, in Dresden, Kirchner, Heckel and Schmidt-Rottluff used thickly-laid vibrant colors to give rein to their own voices, to the anguished expression of their emotions, deforming a world they were unable to accept.

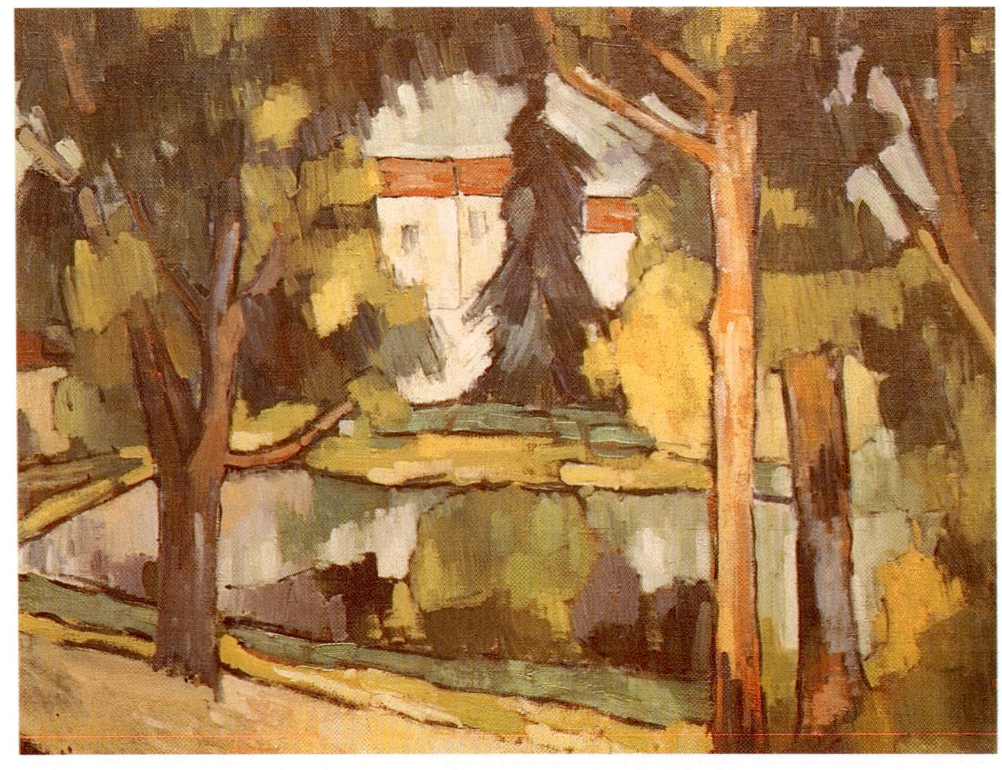

● In France, Van Gogh's lesson was tinged with optimism. His distortions and his non-descriptive use of color became the instruments of a more serene form of research aimed at communication rather than criticism. The *Fauves* group, whose members included Matisse, Derain and Vlaminck, inherited Van Gogh's preference for primary colors, making use of a thickly-applied, even more aggressive layering of paint. By juxtaposing colors squeezed directly from the tube, the French artists depicted reality freely and almost without profundity, with results that were often a prelude to abstract art.

◆ EDWARD MUNCH
The Scream
(1893, Oslo, Kommunes Kunstamlinger Munch Museet).
Among Van Gogh's heirs, no-one was more successful in reproducing the dramatic link between art and life. Munch was influenced not so much by formal elements, but by the existential drama, which he described with a style that was equally dense, although with a darker range of colors.

◆ EMIL NOLDE
The Garden of Trollhois
(1907, Stiftung Seebüll Ada und Emil Nolde).
The panic and highly religious framework that characterizes Nolde's work derives from the example of Van Gogh. Nolde inverts the expressive use of colors, exalting the varied richness of nature.

◆ MAURICE DE VLAMINCK
Le maison de Chatau
(1904, Geneva, private collection).
Vlaminck, whose life was devoid of Van Gogh's dramatic suffering, maintained the same thickly encrusted brush-stroke.
His bright, joyful tones and his naturalistic subjects describe a world of happiness.

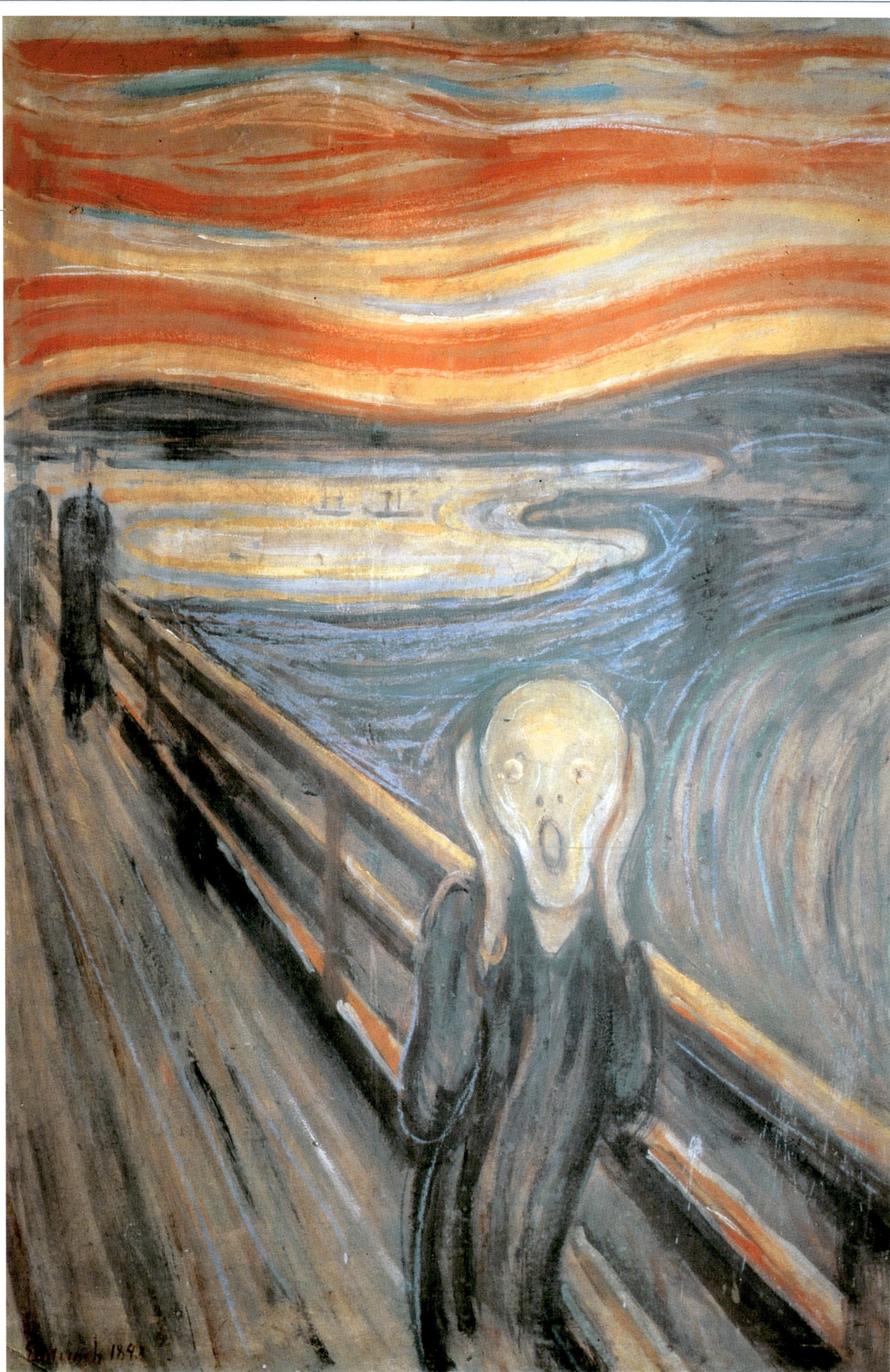

THE ARTISTIC JOURNEY

For a vision of the whole of Van Gogh's prduction, we propose here a chronological reading of his principal works.

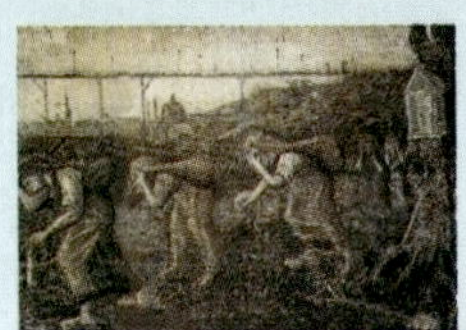

♦ THE LOAD-BEARERS (1881)
The drawing (now at Otterlo) offers a bitter picture of the life of the Borinage miners in Belgium, where the artist stayed for a few months. Their backs bent under the weight and almost deformed in an unnatural position, the workers seem to exorcise their fatigue by invoking the crucifix on the right. The human figures in the foreground contrast with the city in the background.

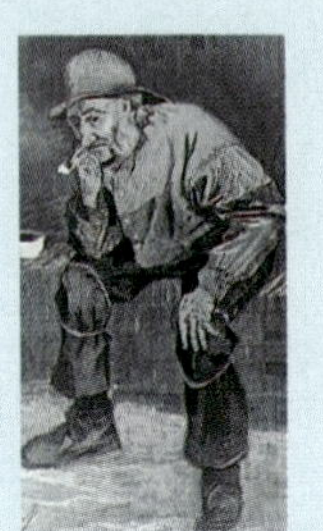

♦ THE OLD FISHERMAN (1883)
The painting (now at Otterlo) is part of a series depicting popular subjects. The strong chiaroscuro and the almost smudged lines accentuate the man's features and cloud his expression. His hat was purchased especially for the occasion, in keeping with a custom that was in fashion at the time among Dutch painters. The thoughtful, absorbed appearance of the fisherman seems to be a reflection of his misery.

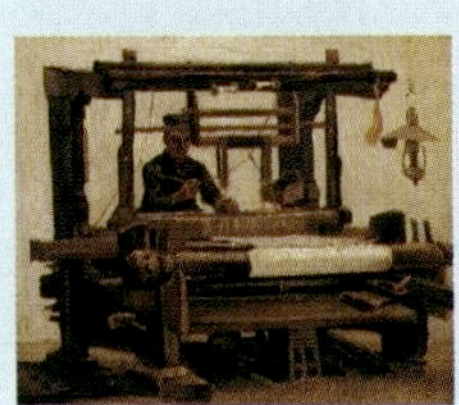

♦ WEAVER, SEEN FROM THE FRONT (1884)
Van Gogh painted this work early in his career, when his main subject was workers. The harshness of their lives is rendered through the dark colors and the coarse features, and in this case through the disproportionate size of the loom compared to the man. The orthogonal grid of the loom somehow frames the figure and draws it visually into its own workings.

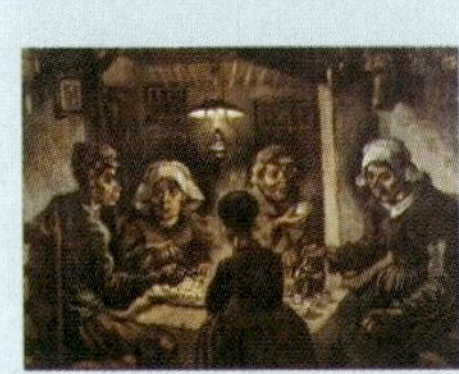

♦ THE POTATO EATERS (1885)
The painting is strongly influenced by the Dutch realist tradition, with dramatic chiaroscuro, dark tones and thick brush-strokes. Van Gogh produced a dozen preparatory drawings, sketching the details and the overall composition. The characters were portrayed separately, which explains the general sense of isolation.

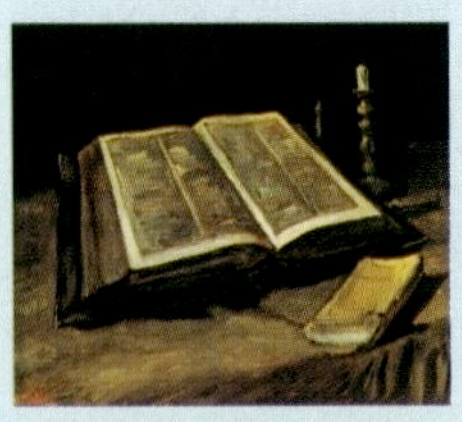

♦ STILL LIFE WITH BIBLE (1885)
In 1885, Reverend Theodorus Van Gogh died suddenly: in this work, the painter describes the tense relationship that linked them. Paternal severity is expressed in the Bible, Van Gogh's rebellious attitude in the novel by Zola. The Bible is open at the passage in Isaiah that recounts the arrival of the servant of God, destined to be rejected. The reference to the artist's own destiny is clear.

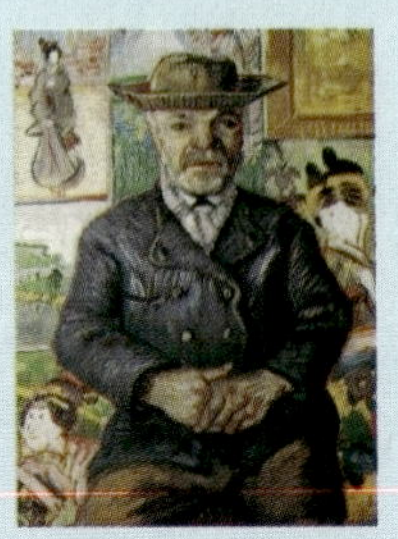

♦ PORTRAIT OF PÈRE TANGUY (1887)
Père Tanguy was a shopkeeper selling artists' materials, much loved by the Impressionists for his straightforward character and also because he was usually prepared to take credit. Van Gogh made two portraits of him, as well as a number of preparatory sketches, always placing him in an exotic Japanese setting. In this work, now in Athens, Tanguy is surrounded by reproductions of Japanese prints. The brush-stroke is rhythmical, the colors bright and flat.

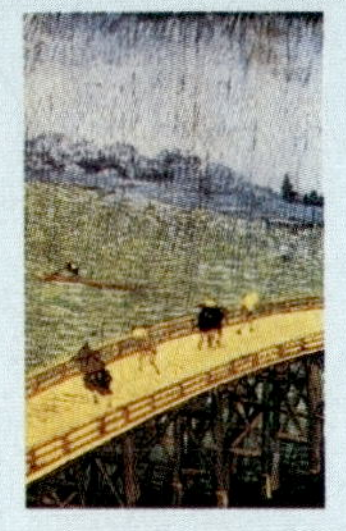

♦ JAPONAISERIE: BRIDGE IN THE RAIN (AFTER HIROSHIGE) (1887)
This is one of the three works painted in Paris from woodcuts by Hiroshige. Van Gogh loved the apparent simplicity of the Japanese work, with its swift strokes and sharp outlines. His version is very different from the original as a result of his unmistakable thick brush-stroke. The painting, was also the inspiration for *Landscape at Auvers in the Rain* (1890).

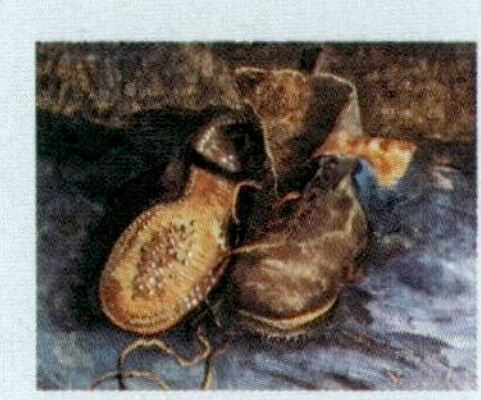

♦ A PAIR OF SHOES (1887)
The subject, which aroused the interest of Heidegger, appears in a series of intense still lifes. The shoes were actually purchased at a second-hand market, in order to be painted, and then worn by Van Gogh until they were dirty enough. The painter used his nails to scratch points of light into the paint, helping to give the image its structure.

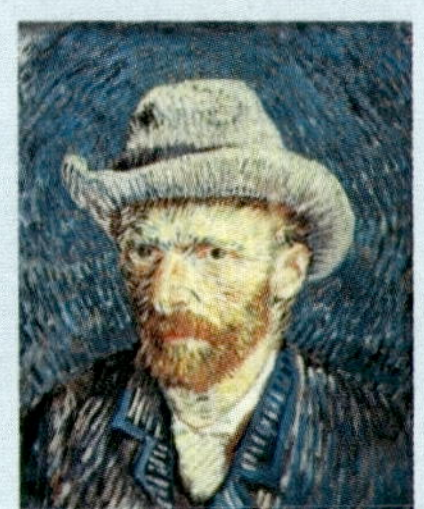

♦ SELF-PORTRAIT (1887)
This self-portrait, in Divisionist style, achieves great communicative power through the use of the extremely close-up angle. Van Gogh was experimenting here with the use of pure colors, especially the primary colors. The segmented brush-strokes spread out around the head like a halo, causing the whole surface of the canvas to vibrate. The shoulders, traced very lightly, are absorbed into the background.

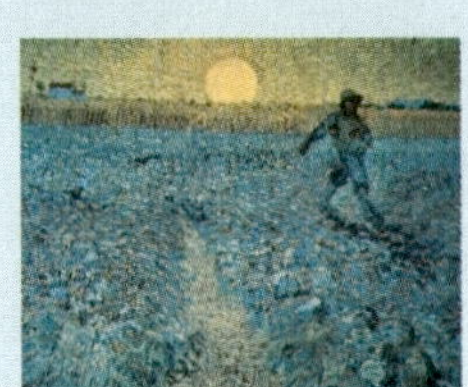

♦ THE SOWER (1888)
Based on Millet's The Sower, the painting opened the cycle that Van Gogh produced in Arles. The high line of the horizon draws the figure into the landscape: the sower, becoming the fulcrum of the composition, lightens the whole. The dazzling juxtaposition of bright colors, the almost musical gesture of the man, the low sun and the city hinted at in the background give the work a symbolic flavor.

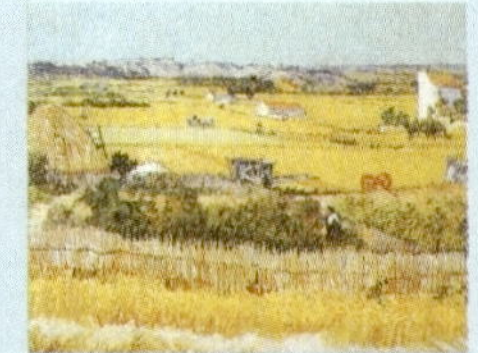

♦ HARVEST AT LA CRAU, WITH MONTMAJOUR IN THE BACKGROUND (1888)
The dynamic center of this painting is the blue cart, placed at the point where the diagonals meet in the middle. The narrative poise with which the landscape is portrayed is overwhelmed by the expressive power of the color yellow, the real protagonist of the painting. Van Gogh creates a remarkable harmony between the primary colors blue and yellow.

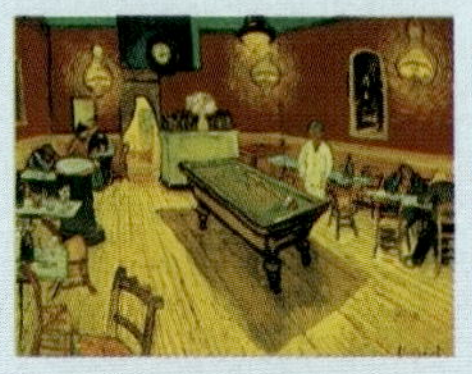

♦ THE NIGHT CAFE IN THE PLACE LAMARTINE IN ARLES (1888)
This canvas is the second attempt to create a symbolic work through the expressive power of color alone. The complementary reds and greens create a rather disturbing visual effect that corresponds to Van Gogh's view of the cafe: "A place where one can come to ruin, go mad, or commit crimes." With this painting the artist responds to a brothel scene sent to him by Emile Bernard.

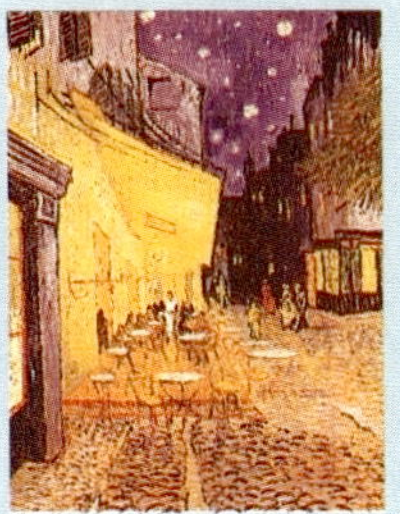

◆ THE CAFE TERRACE ON THE PLACE DU FORUM, ARLES, AT NIGHT (1888)

The painting belongs to the period in Arles in which Van Gogh was interested in night scenes. Here the primary colors continue to dominate. The feeling of serenity is produced through the skilful use of cold tones – the blues that pervade the objects in the shade – and warm tones, which explode with great intensity in the yellows of the terrace.

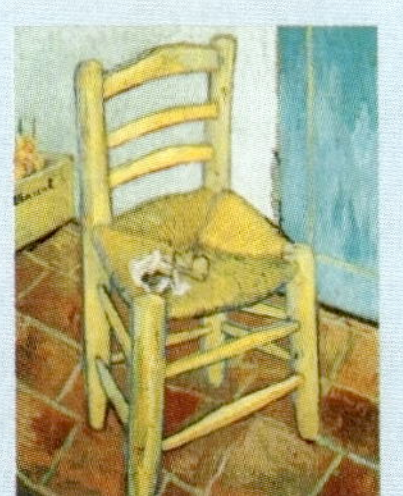

◆ VINCENT'S CHAIR WITH HIS PIPE (1888)

This painting forms a pair with Paul Gauguin's Armchair. Here the subject is depicted in daylight, in a simple, everyday environment. The crooked perspective, the uneven tiles, the corner of the onion box, and the humble nature of the chair itself reproduce the poetry of familiar objects. The pipe and tobacco evoke the artist with the intensity of a slice of real life.

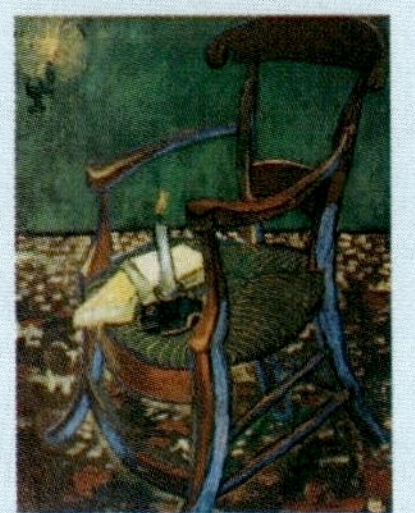

◆ PAUL GAUGUIN'S ARMCHAIR (1888)

The subject is depicted at night, with lamps and candles. The absence of a signature and some of the details of the composition suggest that the work remained unfinished. Although it seems rather unstable, the chair is more elegant than the previous one: the composition is more linear and careful, as we can see from the floor. The expressive use of color also distinguishes this painting from *Vincent's Chair*.

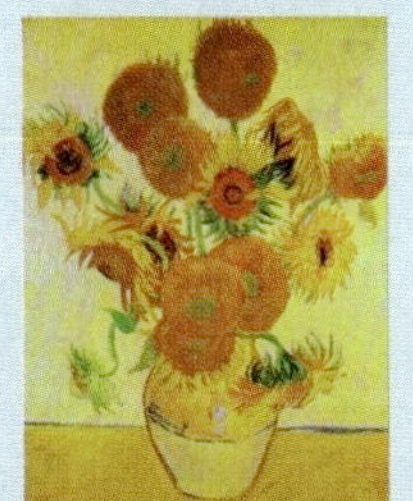

◆ VASE WITH SUNFLOWERS (1889)

Produced in Arles at the time when the artist's work was characterized by the explosion of color and animated by the intense light of Provence, the painting belongs to what is perhaps his most famous cycle. The expressive power of the yellow overwhelms the subject, evoking the brightness of the sun. By tracing the outline of the vase in blue, Van Gogh saves the composition from the risk of seeming flat.

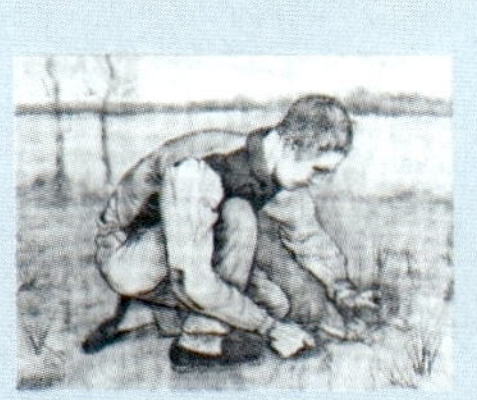

◆ PEASANT WITH SICKLE (1881)

After a long interval, in Arles Van Gogh goes back to reproducing the rural scenes of Millet, for the first time producing copies using color. In the meantime his palette, after his contact with the Impressionists, has lightened, while his brush-stroke has become more knotty and tormented. In this work (now in Amsterdam), the bending pose and the almost deformed outline remind us of the Borinage miners.

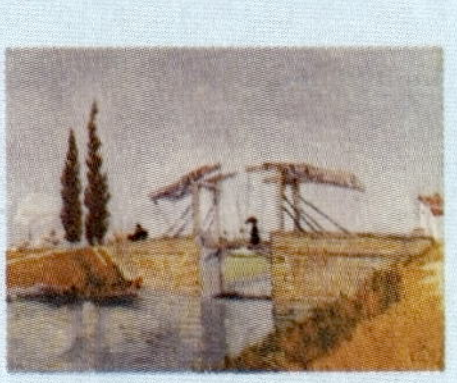

◆ THE LANGLOIS BRIDGE AT ARLES (1889)

This painting belongs to a series of works produced in Arles during the spring. In keeping with Impressionist painting, Van Gogh uses the motif of the bridge to investigate the intensity of the sky and the reflections in the water in relation to the atmospheric light. The colors are pale and transparent. The precision of the brush-stroke and the synthetic composition reveal the influence of Japanese art.

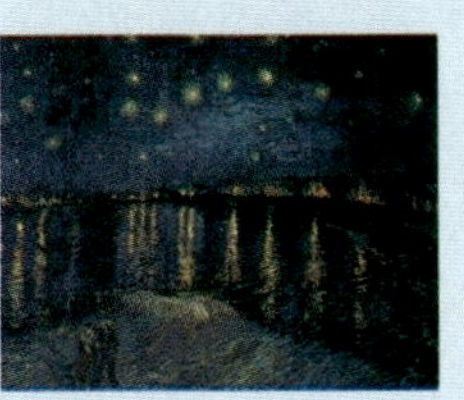

◆ STARRY NIGHT OVER THE RHONE (1889)

The charmed and musical atmosphere recalls the works of Whistler or Monet. Van Gogh simplifies the composition to the extent of abstraction, bringing the shapes to the surface and turning them into patches of color. He plays with the contrast between the night-sky and the artificial lights, using the direction of the brush-strokes to distinguish between the sky, the strip of land on the horizon, and the river.

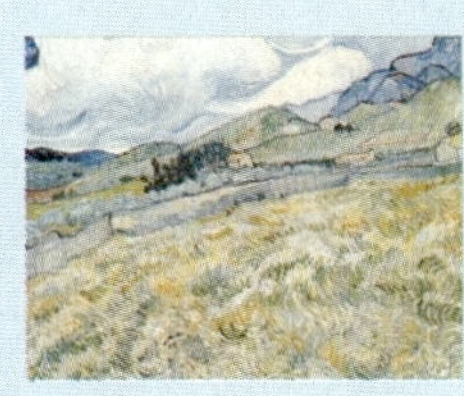

◆ WHEAT FIELD WITH LARGE CLOUD (1889)

The painting was produced during the early part of his time in Saint-Rémy, when he was not allowed to paint outside the bounds of the hospital. The landscape, with the gentle profile of the mountains, the arabesques of the sky, and the wheat undulating in the wind, is observed from his room. The style is highly synthetic, and the colors remain subdued despite the lively, darting brush-strokes.

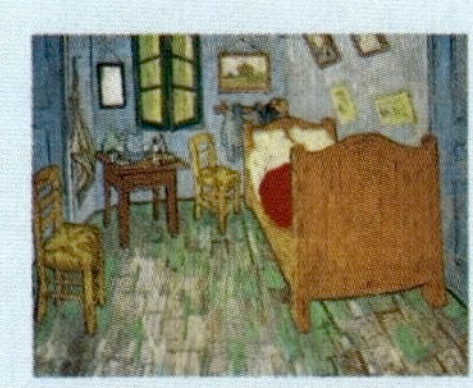

◆ VINCENT'S BEDROOM IN ARLES (1889)

Of the three paintings of the subject, this one has the most deforming perspective. The altered dimensions of the room produce a sort of oscillation. The painting is a copy made in the asylum of the original that is now in Amsterdam. In a letter to Theo, Van Gogh said that he aimed to give the idea of rest, but the arrangement of the objects, scattered around in an unreal space, creates an unsettling effect.

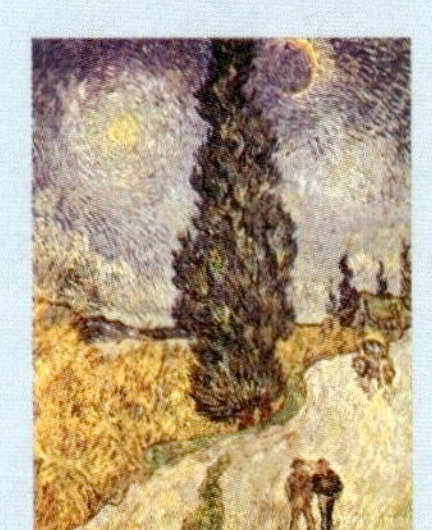

◆ ROAD WITH CYPRESS AND STAR (1890)

Like a tongue of fire, the cypress rises towards the sky, challenging the proportions of the scene. The power of the colors is matched by the energetic brush-stroke, which draws the whole scene into a single vibration. In this transfigured world, Van Gogh depicts a farmhouse, relegated to one side of the painting, a cart, and two small figures on their way home from work along the winding road.

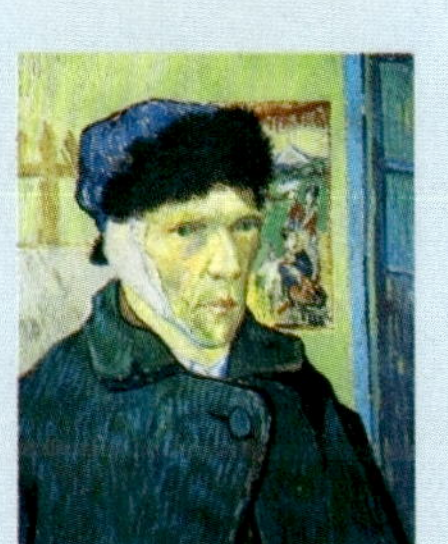

◆ SELF-PORTRAIT WITH BANDAGED EAR (1889)

The painting shows the artist a few weeks after his self-inflicted injury, his expression disconsolate and his ear bandaged. The head, turned to the right, upsets the balance of the composition by highlighting the bandage. The artist portrays himself in his own room as if he were a stranger, a passer-by in a thick coat. Behind him we can make out a Japanese print and an easel.

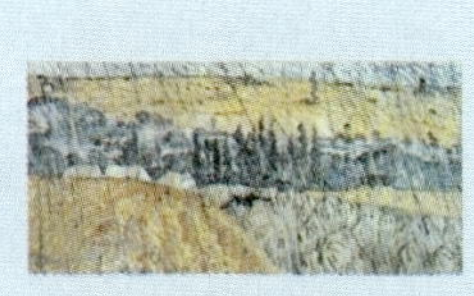

◆ LANDSCAPE AT AUVERS IN THE RAIN (1890)

In this canvas (now in Cardiff), the artist adopts the format of the double rectangle. Using short, uneven brush-strokes, he almost simulates the graininess of wood, reworking the woodcuts of Hiroshige in an original manner. The arrangement of the subject, which stretches lengthways, the extremely high horizon and the rhythm of the cypresses give the desolate landscape a sense of solitude.

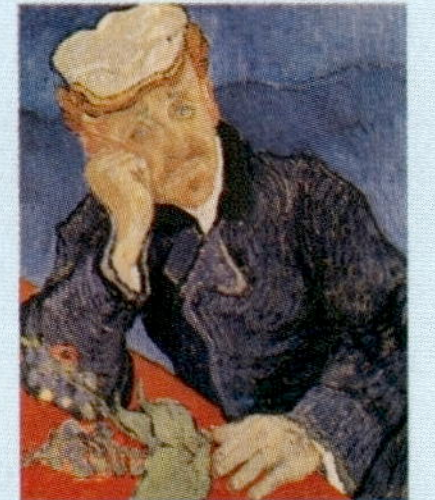

◆ PORTRAIT OF DOCTOR GACHET (1890)

In Auvers Van Gogh painted two portraits of Doctor Gachet, aiming to depict his interior character rather than to produce a physiognomic likeness. The expressive instability of the composition, based on diagonal lines, is accentuated by the synthetic outline of the figure. The perspective intensifies the engrossed, melancholic expression and highlights the foxgloves, a symbol of the medical profession.

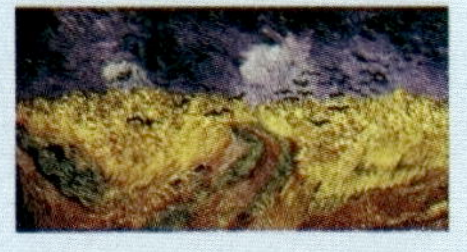

◆ WHEAT FIELD WITH CROWS (1890)

Here Van Gogh takes the simplification of the composition to the extreme, annulling any sense of depth and entrusting the expression of his own anguish to the colors. Using a flat brush, he attacks the canvas with violent strokes. There is no light, no hope in this solitary landscape, swept by the wind beneath the menacing sky.

TO KNOW MORE

The following pages contain: some documents useful for understanding different aspects of Van Gogh's life and work; a brief biography, technical data and locations of the main works and an essential bibliography.

DOCUMENTS AND TESTIMONIES

"My dear brother, it is always in an interval of time that I write to you, I am toiling like a man possessed, I feel more than ever a deaf frenzy of work, and I believe this will help to cure me."

[Vincent Van Gogh to Theo, Saint-Rémy, September 1889]

Painting and excess

Albert Aurier, the Parisian art critic, published an article entitled "Les isolés: Vincent Van Gogh" in the pages of "Mercure de France". It was January 1890, a few months before the artist's suicide. Aurier was one of the few contemporary intellectuals to understand the genius of Van Gogh and to manifest publicly his enthusiasm for the Dutch artist's disturbing, innovative work.

"It is an unusual nature that takes form, unsettling and perturbing, at once truly real and almost supernatural [...]. What characterizes his entire oeuvre is excess. Excess of strength, excess of nerves, the violence of the expression. In his categorical affirmation of the character of things, in his often reckless simplification of forms, in his insolence in looking the sun in the face, in the vehement passion of the design and the color, right down to the smallest details of technique, he shows himself to be potent, masculine, courageous, very often brutal and sometimes naively delicate. [...] And thus how can we explain his obsessive passion for the sun, which shines in his fiery skies, and at the same time for that other sun, the vegetable star, the sumptuous sunflower, which he paints tirelessly, like a maniac, how can we explain it if we refuse to admit his persistent concern with some vague and glorious helio-mythical allegory?"

"He had not allowed himself to be absorbed by nature; rather, he had absorbed it within himself; he had forced it to bend, to shape itself according to the forms of his thought, to follow his visions, even to suffer his peculiar deformations [...]. Van Gogh had, to a very rare degree, the talent that distinguishes one man from another: style."

[Octave Mirbeau, "Echo de Paris", 31 March 1890]

"This man will either go mad or leave us all a long way behind."

[Camille Pissarro]

Yellow to warm the soul

With impatience though with great insight, Paul Gauguin recalls his relationship with his difficult colleague.

"In a way, one could feel the imminence of a clash between our very different natures, one of them volcanic, the other equally restless but more collected. In everything and everywhere I found a disorder that annoyed me. The paint box was overflowing with squeezed tubes, always without their tops, and despite the disorder and the chaos, a special harmony flowed from the canvas. As it did from his words. [...] Oh yes! He loved yellow, the rays of sun that warmed the soul, the good Vincent, this painter from Holland who hated the fog. It was his desperate need for warmth."

"I will be an arbitrary colorist"

In this letter to his brother Theo, Vincent reiterates his devotion to the land, and in his portraits of the peasants in Arles he rediscovered his tie with the tradition of the pre-Impressionist painters. He cites writers of social realism, but seeks a new form of expression in the free use of color.

"My dear Theo, very soon you will meet Messer Patience Escalier, a man of the fields, an old cowherd of the Camargue, now the gardener in a farmhouse on the Crau. Later today I will send you the drawing I made from that study, and also the drawing of the portrait of the postman Roulin.

The color of this portrait of a peasant is less dark than that of the *Potato Eaters* from Nuenen, but the refined Parisian *Portier*, probably so called because he throws paintings out of the door, will find the same question to resolve. Now you have changed, but you will see he has not changed, and it is a real shame that in Paris there are not more paintings *in clogs*. I do not think my peasant will come out badly next to the Lautrec you have, for example, and I actually think that the Lautrec will immediately become more distinct, by contrast, and mine too will benefit from the strange juxtaposition, because the skin burnt and tanned by the strong sun and by the open air will stand out all the more next to the rice powder and the elegant toilette. What a pity that the Parisians do not appreciate rustic things, Monticelli, the pumpkin, anyway I know one should not despair, because a utopia never becomes reality. Only, I find that what I learned in Paris *disappears* and I return to the ideas that came to me in the countryside before I met the Impressionists. I would not be at all astonished if the Impressionists didn't have some objections to make, very soon, about my way of painting, which has been influenced more by the ideas of Delacroix than by theirs.

Because instead of trying to render exactly that which I see before me, I use color in a more arbitrary way to express myself with intensity. Anyway, let us forget theories: I want to give you an example of what I mean. I would like to paint the portrait of an artist friend, who dreams great dreams, who works as a nightingale sings, because this is his nature. This man should be blond. And I would like to put the esteem and the love I feel for him in the painting. I would thus portray him as he is, as faithfully as possible, to begin with. But the painting would not be finished. To complete it I will be an arbitrary colorist. I will exaggerate the blondness of the hair, even using orange tones, chrome yellow, pale lemon. Behind his head, instead of painting the

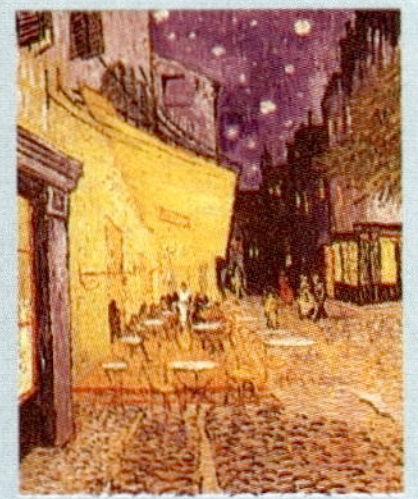

◆ **THE CAFE TERRACE ON THE PLACE DU FORUM, ARLES, AT NIGHT (1888)**
The painting belongs to the period in Arles in which Van Gogh was interested in night scenes. Here the primary colors continue to dominate. The feeling of serenity is produced through the skilful use of cold tones – the blues that pervade the objects in the shade – and warm tones, which explode with great intensity in the yellows of the terrace.

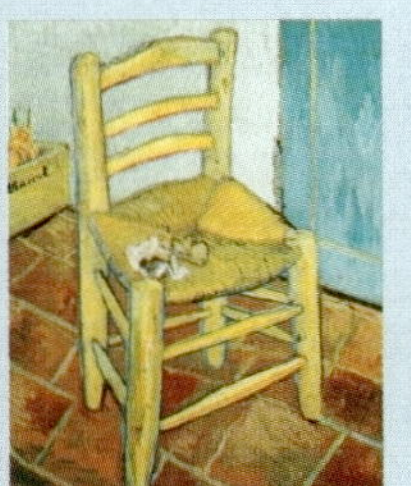

◆ **VINCENT'S CHAIR WITH HIS PIPE (1888)**
This painting forms a pair with Paul Gauguin's Armchair. Here the subject is depicted in daylight, in a simple, everyday environment. The crooked perspective, the uneven tiles, the corner of the onion box, and the humble nature of the chair itself reproduce the poetry of familiar objects. The pipe and tobacco evoke the artist with the intensity of a slice of real life.

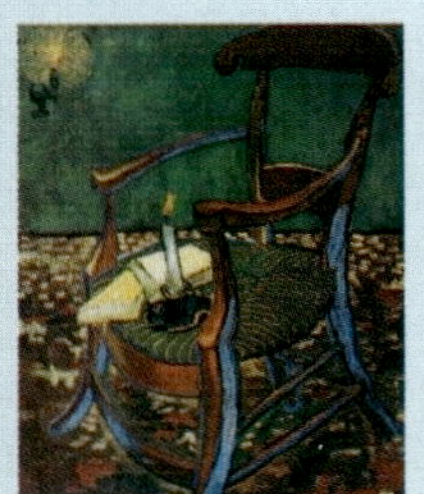

◆ **PAUL GAUGUIN'S ARMCHAIR (1888)**
The subject is depicted at night, with lamps and candles. The absence of a signature and some of the details of the composition suggest that the work remained unfinished. Although it seems rather unstable, the chair is more elegant than the previous one: the composition is more linear and careful, as we can see from the floor. The expressive use of color also distinguishes this painting from *Vincent's Chair*.

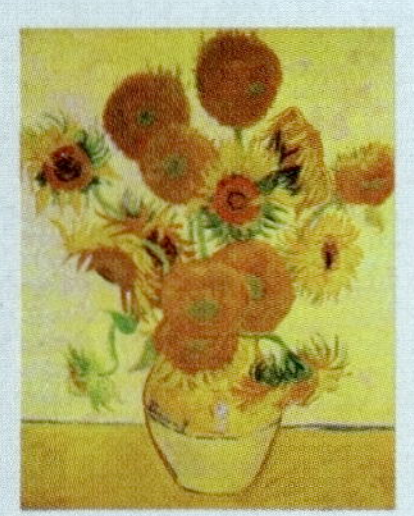

◆ **VASE WITH SUNFLOWERS (1889)**
Produced in Arles at the time when the artist's work was characterized by the explosion of color and animated by the intense light of Provence, the painting belongs to what is perhaps his most famous cycle. The expressive power of the yellow overwhelms the subject, evoking the brightness of the sun. By tracing the outline of the vase in blue, Van Gogh saves the composition from the risk of seeming flat.

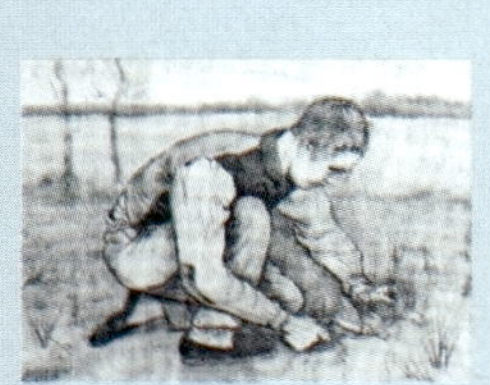

◆ **PEASANT WITH SICKLE (1881)**
After a long interval, in Arles Van Gogh goes back to reproducing the rural scenes of Millet, for the first time producing copies using color. In the meantime his palette, after his contact with the Impressionists, has lightened, while his brush-stroke has become more knotty and tormented. In this work (now in Amsterdam), the bending pose and the almost deformed outline remind us of the Borinage miners.

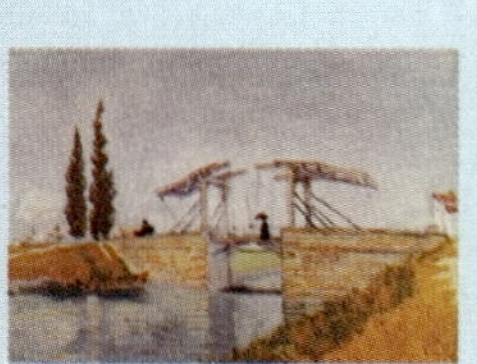

◆ **THE LANGLOIS BRIDGE AT ARLES (1889)**
This painting belongs to a series of works produced in Arles during the spring. In keeping with Impressionist painting, Van Gogh uses the motif of the bridge to investigate the intensity of the sky and the reflections in the water in relation to the atmospheric light. The colors are pale and transparent. The precision of the brush-stroke and the synthetic composition reveal the influence of Japanese art.

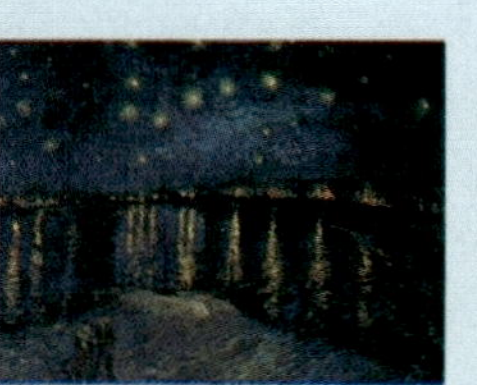

◆ **STARRY NIGHT OVER THE RHONE (1889)**
The charmed and musical atmosphere recalls the works of Whistler or Monet. Van Gogh simplifies the composition to the extent of abstraction, bringing the shapes to the surface and turning them into patches of color. He plays with the contrast between the night-sky and the artificial lights, using the direction of the brush-strokes to distinguish between the sky, the strip of land on the horizon, and the river.

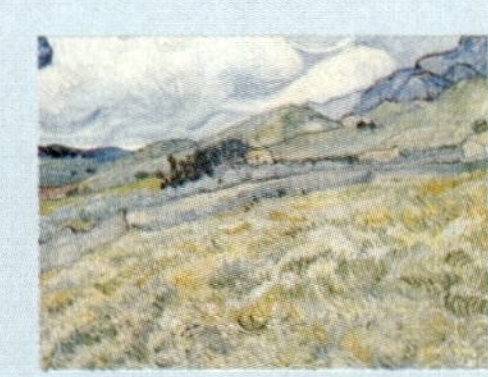

◆ **WHEAT FIELD WITH LARGE CLOUD (1889)**
The painting was produced during the early part of his time in Saint-Rémy, when he was not allowed to paint outside the bounds of the hospital. The landscape, with the gentle profile of the mountains, the arabesques of the sky, and the wheat undulating in the wind, is observed from his room. The style is highly synthetic, and the colors remain subdued despite the lively, darting brush-strokes.

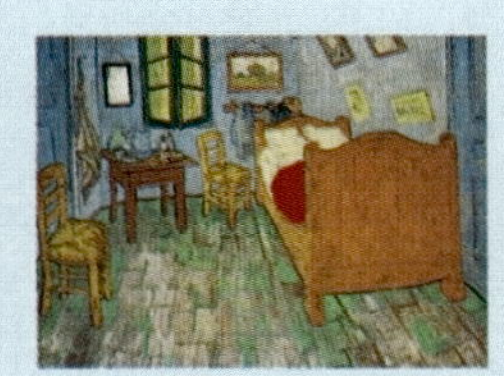

◆ **VINCENT'S BEDROOM IN ARLES (1889)**
Of the three paintings of the subject, this one has the most deforming perspective. The altered dimensions of the room produce a sort of oscillation. The painting is a copy made in the asylum of the original that is now in Amsterdam. In a letter to Theo, Van Gogh said that he aimed to give the idea of rest, but the arrangement of the objects, scattered around in an unreal space, creates an unsettling effect.

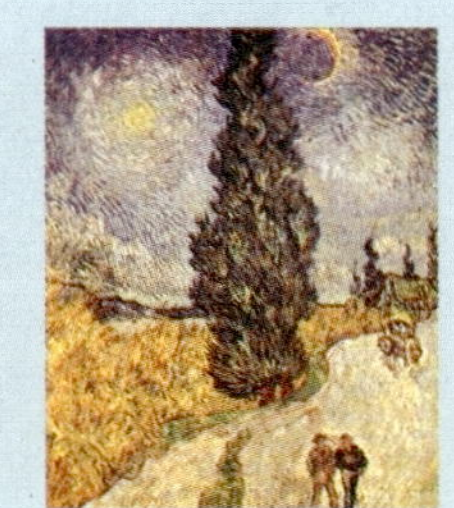

◆ **ROAD WITH CYPRESS AND STAR (1890)**
Like a tongue of fire, the cypress rises towards the sky, challenging the proportions of the scene. The power of the colors is matched by the energetic brush-stroke, which draws the whole scene into a single vibration. In this transfigured world, Van Gogh depicts a farmhouse, relegated to one side of the painting, a cart, and two small figures on their way home from work along the winding road.

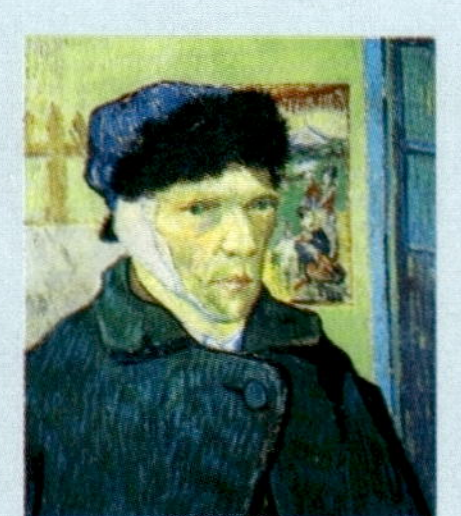

◆ **SELF-PORTRAIT WITH BANDAGED EAR (1889)**
The painting shows the artist a few weeks after his self-inflicted injury, his expression disconsolate and his ear bandaged. The head, turned to the right, upsets the balance of the composition by highlighting the bandage. The artist portrays himself in his own room as if he were a stranger, a passer-by in a thick coat. Behind him we can make out a Japanese print and an easel.

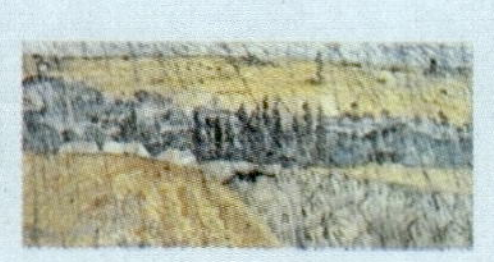

◆ **LANDSCAPE AT AUVERS IN THE RAIN (1890)**
In this canvas (now in Cardiff), the artist adopts the format of the double rectangle. Using short, uneven brush-strokes, he almost simulates the graininess of wood, reworking the woodcuts of Hiroshige in an original manner. The arrangement of the subject, which stretches lengthways, the extremely high horizon and the rhythm of the cypresses give the desolate landscape a sense of solitude.

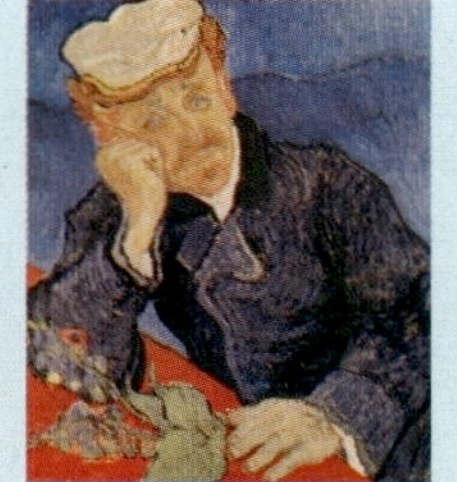

◆ **PORTRAIT OF DOCTOR GACHET (1890)**
In Auvers Van Gogh painted two portraits of Doctor Gachet, aiming to depict his interior character rather than to produce a physiognomic likeness. The expressive instability of the composition, based on diagonal lines, is accentuated by the synthetic outline of the figure. The perspective intensifies the engrossed, melancholic expression and highlights the foxgloves, a symbol of the medical profession.

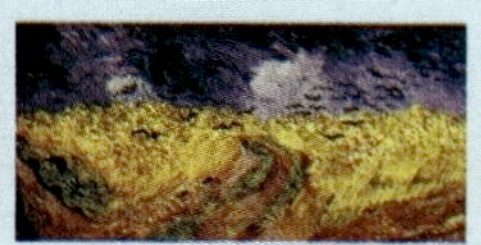

◆ **WHEAT FIELD WITH CROWS (1890)**
Here Van Gogh takes the simplification of the composition to the extreme, annulling any sense of depth and entrusting the expression of his own anguish to the colors. Using a flat brush, he attacks the canvas with violent strokes. There is no light, no hope in this solitary landscape, swept by the wind beneath the menacing sky.

ordinary wall of the miserable apartment, I will paint infinity, I will make a simple background of the richest blue, as intense as I can achieve; from this simple combination, the blond head lit up against this sumptuous blue, comes a mysterious effect like a star in the deep blue.
In the portrait of the peasant I followed the same system. And yet without aiming in this case to evoke the mysterious splendor of a pale star. But imagining the terrible man I had to do in the middle of harvest time, at midday. This explains the blazing oranges like burning iron, the tones like old gold glowing in the shadows.
Ah, dear brother... in these exaggerations the right-minded will only find caricature.
But what does it matter, we have read *La Terre* and *Germinal*, and if we paint a peasant, we would like to show that this reading has left an effect on us.
I don't know if I will be able to paint the postman *as I feel him*, this man resembles Père Tanguy, as a revolutionary, he is probably thought of as a good Republican, because he detests in a cordial manner the republic whose benefits we enjoy, and because overall he doubts and is rather disenchanted by the very idea of the republic. But one day I saw him as he was singing the Marseillaise, and I felt I was seeing 1789, not the year after, but that very year 99 years ago. It was Delacroix, Daumier, the old Dutch masters. Unfortunately I can't get him to pose, although it would be necessary to do a painting, an intelligent model.
I have to tell you that these days are extremely hard from a material point of view. Whatever I do life is very expensive, almost like in Paris, where I would spend four or five francs a day, without doing anything special. I use models, and so it becomes even more difficult. It doesn't matter, I will carry on like this all the same. Just as I assure you that if you could see your way to sending a little money now and then, the paintings would benefit, and not me. On my part I only have the choice between being a good painter and being a mediocre painter. I choose the former. But the needs of painting are like those of an expensive mistress, one can do nothing without money and one never has enough. And so painting must be done at the expense of society and not be a burden on the artist, but on the other hand one should keep quiet, because *nobody forces you to work*, given that indifference towards painting is fatally universal, and has been for a long time.
Fortunately my stomach has settled to the extent that I have lived for three weeks a month on seafood, with milk and eggs.
It is the wonderful heat that restores my strength, and I was certainly not wrong to come straight to the South without waiting for my illness to become incurable. Yes, I am now as well as other people, which has only happened for brief periods in Nuenen, for example, and this is anything but displeasing.
When I say other people, I mean the diggers, Père Tanguy, Père Millet, the peasants: when one is well one should be able to live on a piece of bread, even when working all day, and still having the strength to smoke and have a drink. And at the same time one should be able to feel clearly that the stars and infinity exist. And so life becomes almost enchanted. Ah, those who do not believe in the sun down here are godless.
Unfortunately, the sun sent by the good God is accompanied three-quarters of the time by a hellish *mistral*.
Saturday's post, God willing, is now passed, I did not doubt that I would receive your letter, but as you see I did not fret about it.
A handshake

yours, Vincent

[Vincent Van Gogh to Theo, Arles, 11 August 1888]

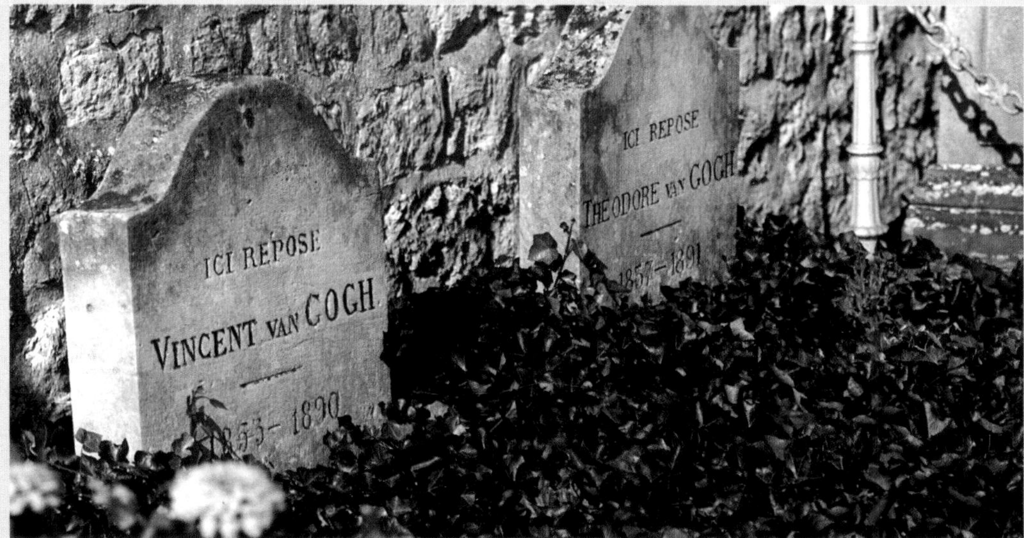

HIS LIFE IN BRIEF

1853. Van Gogh is born on 30 March in Groot-Zundert (Holland). He is given the name of the brother who died a year earlier. His father is a Protestant preacher, and brings him up strictly.
1864. Attends the college of Zevenvergen, where he studies English, French and German, and begins to draw.
1869. Begins his apprenticeship in The Hague, in the local branch of the Parisian workshop Goupil & Cie. He remains there until 1876, staying for a long time in London.
1875. Moves to Paris, where he had been the previous year. He visits museums and galleries, and goes through a strongly religious phase.
1876. Returns to London as a teacher, and gives his first sermon. Decides to devote his life to evangelizing the poor.
1878-80. Rejected by the Faculty of Theology in Amsterdam, he pursues the vocation of lay preacher, living in poverty and spending his time among sick people and miners. He draws scenes based on these experiences and begins to copy the works of Millet.
1882. Moves to The Hague, where he takes painting lessons from Mauve. Paints mainly landscapes and sketches of popular life.
1884-85. Lives in Nuenen for two years. Paints numerous landscapes and scenes of workers (weavers and peasants), characterized by dark, earthy colors. Paints *The Potato Eaters*. In Amsterdam he is influenced by Rembrandt and Hals, while in Antwerp he is struck by the work of Rubens. Buys his first Japanese engravings.
1886. Returns to Paris and meets Toulouse-Lautrec and Gauguin, with whom he exhibits the following year. Thanks to his encounter with the Impressionists, his paintings become lighter and more luminous. He adopts the *pointilliste* brush-stroke of Seurat. Paints over 200 canvases. Buys more Japanese prints.
1888. Moves to Arles. Paints peaceful landscapes and his first sunflowers. In October Gauguin joins him, staying until 23 December, when Gogh cuts off part of his left ear.
1889. Spends a long time in hospital, possessed by hallucinations. From May lives in an asylum in Saint-Rémy. Alternates violent fits with moments of calm. Paints numerous cypresses.
1890. In January takes part in the exhibition "Les Vingt" in Brussels; in February exhibits at the Salon des Indépendants in Paris. In May moves to Auvers-sur-Oise, where he is looked after by Doctor Gachet, a friend of the Impressionists and an amateur painter. On 27 July, during a walk, he shoots himself. Dies during the night two days later.

WHERE TO SEE VAN GOGH

Below is a list of the major works by Van Gogh housed in public collections. The list is arranged according to the cities where they are found. The following information is given: title, date, technique and support, measurements in centimeters.

AMSTERDAM (HOLLAND)
The Potato Eaters, 1885; oil on canvas, 82 x 114; Rijksmuseum Van Gogh.

Still Life with Bible, 1885; oil on canvas, 65 x 78; Rijksmuseum Van Gogh.

Agostina Segatori Sitting at the "Café du Tambourin", 1887; oil on canvas, 55.5 x 46.5; Rijksmuseum Van Gogh.

Self-Portrait, 1887; oil on canvas, 44 x 37.5; Rijksmuseum Van Gogh.

Vincent's House in Arles (The Yellow House), 1888; oil on canvas, 76 x 94; Rijksmuseum Van Gogh.

Paul Gauguin's Armchair, 1888; oil on canvas, 90.5 x 72; Rijksmuseum Van Gogh.

Wheatfield with Crows, 1890, oil on canvas, 50.5 x 100.5; Rijksmuseum Van Gogh.

Irises, 1890; oil on canvas, 92 x 73.5; Rijksmuseum Van Gogh.

Blossoming Almond Tree, 1890; oil on canvas, 73 x 92; Rijksmuseum Van Gogh.

BOSTON (UNITED STATES)
Portrait of the Postman Joseph Roulin, 1888, oil on canvas, 81 x 65; Museum of Fine Arts.

CHICAGO (UNITED STATES)
Vincent's Bedroom in Arles, 1889; oil on canvas, 73 x 92; Art Institute.

COLOGNE (GERMANY)
The Langlois Bridge at Arles, 1888; oil on canvas, 49.5 x 64; Wallraf-Richartz Museum.

LONDON (ENGLAND)
Vincent's Chair with his Pipe, 1888; oil on canvas, 93 x 73,5; National Gallery.

Still Life with Sunflowers, 1888; oil on canvas, 93 x 73; National Gallery.

MUNICH (GERMANY)
Vase with Twelve Sunflowers, 1888; oil on canvas, 91 x 72; Neue Pinakothek.

Tree Trunks with View of Arles, 1889; oil on canvas, 72 x 92; Neue Pinakothek.

NEW HAVEN (UNITED STATES)
The Night Cafe in the Place Lamartine in Arles, 1888; oil on canvas, 70 x 89; Yale University Art Gallery.

NEW YORK (UNITED STATES)
Cypresses, 1889; oil on canvas, 95 x 73; Metropolitan Museum of Art.

Portrait of Doctor Gachet, 1890; oil on canvas, 66 x 57; S. Kramarsky Trust Fund.

OTTERLO (HOLLAND)
Weaver, Seen from the Front, 1884; oil on canvas, 70 x 85; Rijksmuseum Kröller-Müller.

Interior of a Restaurant, 1887; oil on canvas, 45.5 x 56.5; Rijksmuseum Kröller-Müller.

The Cafe Terrace on the Place du Forum, Arles, at Night, 1888; oil on canvas, 81 x 65.5; Rijksmuseum Kröller-Müller.

The Sower, 1888; oil on canvas, 64 x 80.5; Rijksmuseum Kröller-Müller.

The Good Samaritan (after Delacroix), 1890, oil on canvas, 73 x 60; Rijksmuseum Kröller-Müller.

Road with Cypress and Star, 1890; oil on canvas, 92 x 73; Rijksmuseum Kröller-Müller.

PARIS (FRANCE)
Self-Portrait, 1889, oil on canvas, 65 x 54; Musée D'Orsay.

Farmhouses in Cordeville, 1890; oil on canvas, 72 x 91; Musée D'Orsay.

The Church at Auvers, 1890; oil on canvas, 94 x 74; Musée D'Orsay.

ROME (ITALY)
L'Arlesienne (Madame Ginoux), 1890; oil on canvas, 61 x 50; Galleria Nazionale d'Arte Moderna.

WASHINGTON (UNITED STATES)
La Musmé, Sitting, 1888; oil on canvas, 74 x 60; National Gallery of Art.

BIBLIOGRAPHY

Readers should consult the general catalogs of the work of Van Gogh in order to get a better idea of the periods that characterized his development.

1923 Paul Gauguin, *Avant et après,* Crès, Paris

1927 Jacop Boart de la Faille, *L'époque française de Van Gogh,* Paris

1928-30 Jacop Boart de la Faille, *L'oeuvre de Vincent Van Gogh, catalogue raisonné,* Bruxelles-Paris

1947 Antonin Artaud, *Van Gogh, Le suicidé de la société,* Paris

1950 Meyer Schapiro, *Vincent Van Gogh,* New York

1953 *Verzamelde Brieven van Vincent van Gogh, uitgegeven en toegelicht door zijn schoonzuster J. van Gogh-Bonger,* Amsterdam-Anversa

1956 John Rewald, *Post-Impressionism, from Van Gogh to Gauguin,* New York

1970 Lionello Venturi, *La via dell'Impressionismo,* Torino

1971 Paolo Lecaldano, *Tutta la pittura di Van Gogh,* 2 vols., Rizzoli, Milano

1986 Dino Formaggio, *Van Gogh in cammino,* Unicopli, Milano

1987 Pascal Bonafoux, *Van Gogh, le soleil en face,* Gallimard, Paris

1988 Ronald De Leeuw, *Van Gogh,* Giunti, Firenze

1989 Melissa McQuillan, *Van Gogh,* London, Thames and Hudson

1990 G. Testori, L. Arigoni, *Van Gogh, Catalogo completo,* Firenze

1994 I. Walther, R. Metzger, *Van Gogh, Complete Paintings,* 2 vols., Taschen, Köln

1995 Gloria Fossi, *Sulle tracce di Van Gogh,* Firenze, Giunti

1996 Various authors, Van Gogh, Giunti Multimedia-La Repubblica, CD-Rom

ONE HUNDRED PAINTINGS:

every one a masterpiece

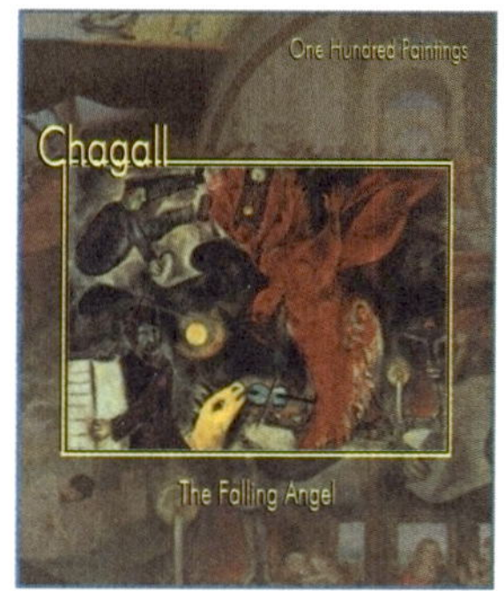

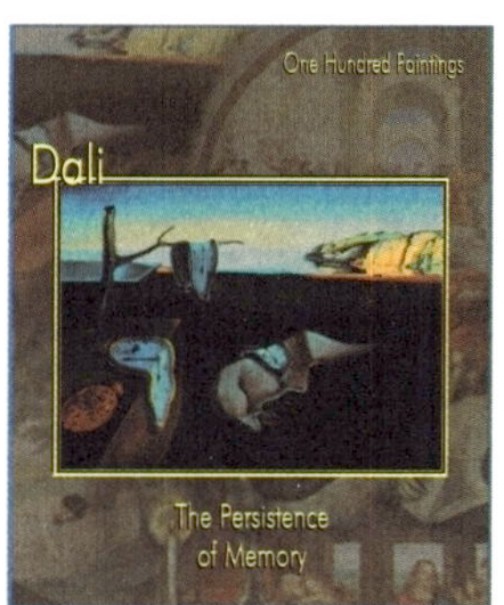

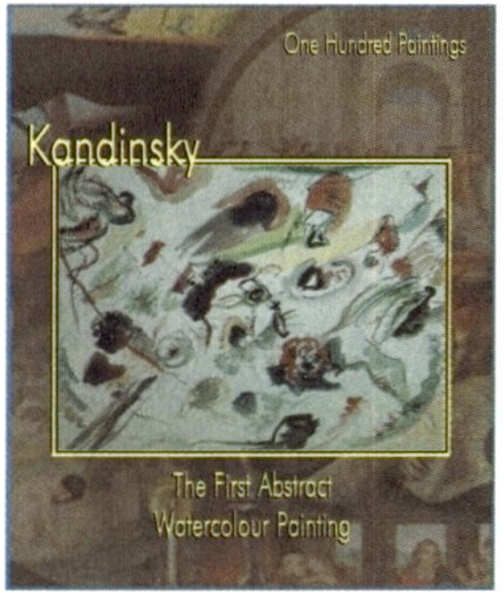

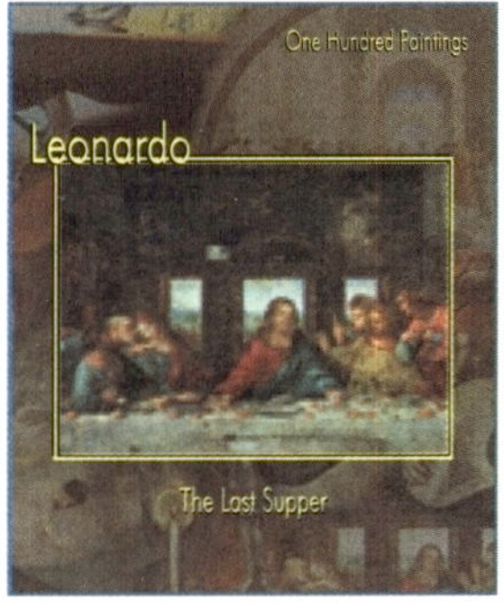

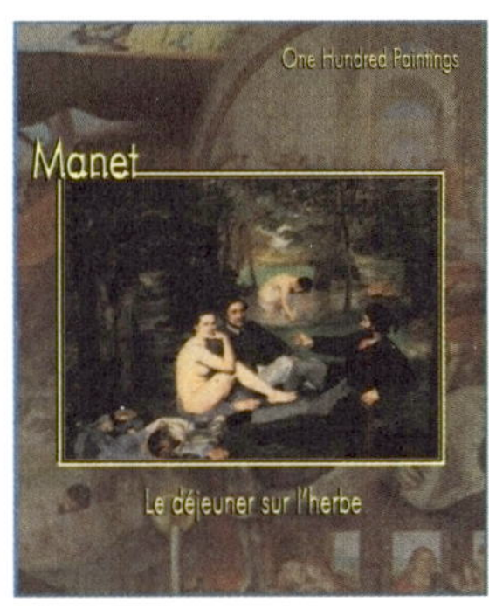

The Work of Art. Which one would it be?

...It is of the works that everyone of you has in mind that I will speak of in "One Hundred Paintings". Together we will analyse the works with regard to the history, the technique, and the hidden aspects in order to discover all that is required to create a particular painting and to produce an artist in general.

It is a way of coming to understand the sensibility and personality of the creator and the tastes, inclinations and symbolisms of the age. The task of "One Hundred Paintings" will therefore be to uncover, together with you, these meanings, to resurrect them from oblivion or to decipher them if they are not immediately perceivable. A painting by Raffaello and one by Picasso have different codes of reading determined not only by the personality of each of the two artists but also the belonging to a different society that have left their unmistakable mark on the work of art. Both paintings impact our senses with force. Our eyes are blinded by the light, by the colour, by the beauty of style, by the glancing look of a character or by the serenity of all of this as a whole. The mind asks itself about the motivations that have led to the works' execution and it tries to grasp all the meanings or messages that the work of art contains.

"One Hundred Paintings" will become your personal collection. From every painting that we analyse you will discover aspects that you had ignored but that instead complete to make the work of art a masterpiece.

Federico Zeri

Coming next in the series:

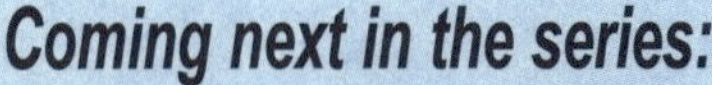

Matisse, Magritte, Titian, Degas, Vermeer, Schiele, Klimt, Poussin, Botticelli, Fussli, Munch, Bocklin, Pontormo, Modigliani, Toulouse-Lautrec, Bosch, Watteau, Arcimboldi, Cezanne, Redon

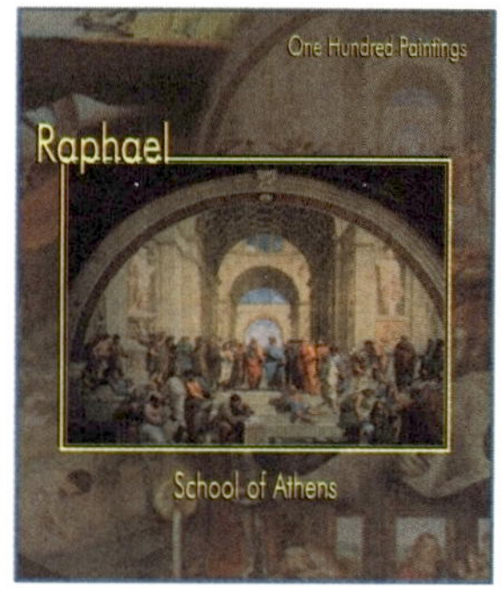

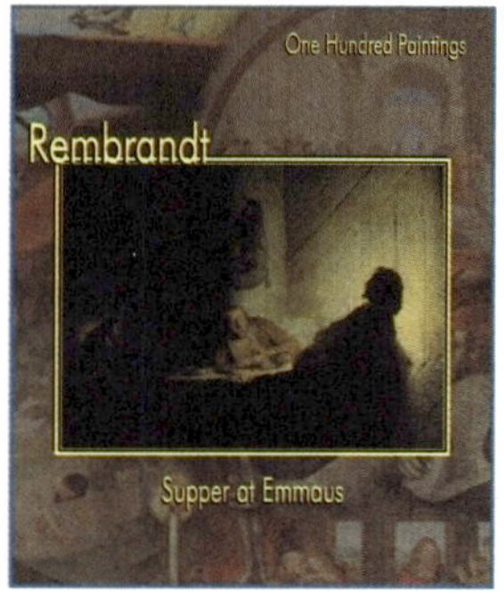

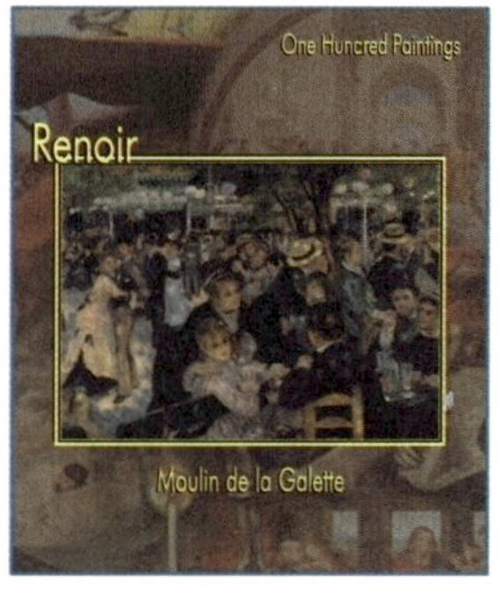

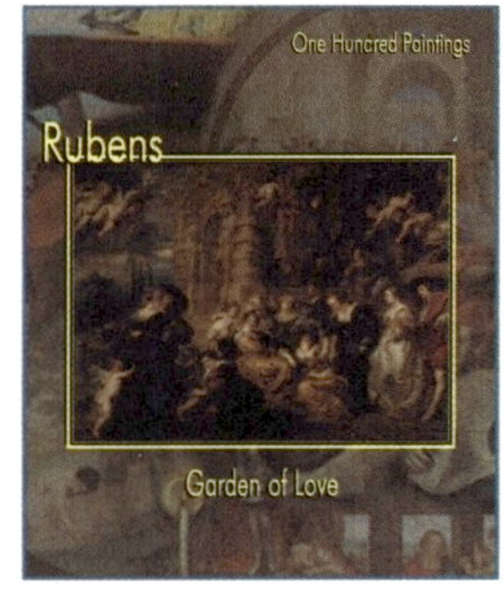

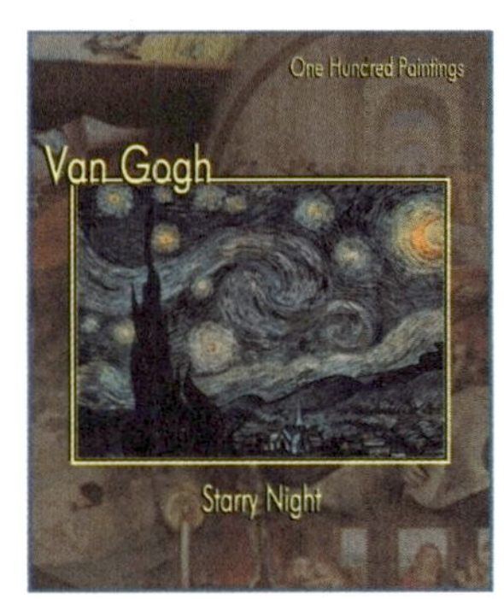